Along Oriskany & Big Creeks

GEOLOGY, HISTORY AND PEOPLE

RICHARD L. WILLIAMS

Charleston   London

THE
History
PRESS

Published by The History Press
Charleston, SC   29403
www.historypress.net

Copyright © 2011 by Richard L.Williams
All rights reserved

Front cover images: Courtesy of Waterville Historical Society and Marc R. Goldberg.
Back cover images: Courtesy of Clinton Historical Society.

First published 2011

Manufactured in the United States

ISBN 978.1.60949.069.0

Library of Congress Cataloging-in-Publication Data

Williams, Richard.
Along Oriskany and Big creeks : geology, history and people / Richard Williams.
p. cm.
Includes bibliographical references and index.
ISBN 978-1-60949-069-0
1. Oriskany Valley (Oneida County and Madison County, N.Y.)--History. 2. Geology--New
York (State)--Oriskany Valley (Oneida County and Madison County) I. Title.
F127.O85W55 2011
974.7'62--dc22
2011005777

Notice: The information in this book is true and complete to the best of our knowledge. It is
offered without guarantee on the part of the author or The History Press. The author and
The History Press disclaim all liability in connection with the use of this book.
All rights reserved. No part of this book may be reproduced or transmitted in any form
whatsoever without prior written permission from the publisher except in the case of brief
quotations embodied in critical articles and reviews.

Contents

Acknowledgements   5

Introduction   7

1. The Oriskany Creek Watershed Changes   9
2. The Stream, Creek, the Falls and Its Tributaries   17
3. The Geology under and at the Sides of the Creek   21
4. Fauna and Flora   27
5. Indians of the Creek and Valley   33
6. Military History   39
7. The Upper Reaches of the Valley   43
8. The Middle Communities   79
9. The Run to the Mohawk   109
10. Economy of the Valley   123

Conclusion   131
Appendix   133
Bibliography   135
Index   139
About the Author   143

Acknowledgements

Any book project requires help from many people and institutions, and this book is no exception. Research was accomplished at these local historical societies: the Clinton Historical Society, Limestone Ridge Historical Society, Waterville Historical Society, Clark Mills Historical Society, Marshall Historical Society and the Oriskany Museum.

The Oneida County Historical Society in Utica has extensive materials in its collection, and they were used during research.

To photographer Marc Goldberg, for producing technically superb pictures; I am indebted, as will be the readers. Older pictures were scanned from private and society collections and some publications. Local public historians were extremely helpful and provided much information about their respective towns and villages: Mabel Bushee (Sangerfield), Phillipa Brown (Waterville), Dorothy McConnell (Marshall), Helen Alberding (Augusta), Diane Van Slyke (Madison), Shirley Hooson (Clark Mills Historical Society), Karen Jacobson (Oriskany Museum) and Shirley Burtch (Oriskany).

My wife, Jean, proofread the manuscript and always made important suggestions for grammar, spelling and punctuation improvements.

I thank the Clinton Historical Society, for its sponsoring and marketing of the book; without its help, it could not have been accomplished.

Clinton artist Tim Pryputniewicz did a fine job on a map of the valley. Hamilton College geology professor emeritus Donald B. Potter has extensive knowledge of the geology of the Oriskany Valley and was the only logical person to write that section. Our fishing expert and sports columnist, John Pitarresi of the *Observer-Dispatch*, provided the part on fishing in the Oriskany.

Finally, I thank Jim Cunningham for his pictures and his clear explanation of the Chenango Canal summit artificial lakes and how their waters today supply the Erie Canal via Oriskany Creek. Jim Cunningham is president of NWT, Inc., an environmental management company, which manages the majority of the water and wastewater facilities in the Oriskany Creek watershed. He is the president of the New York State Federation of Lakes, the president of Madison County Federation of Lakes and a coauthor of *Diet for a Small Lake*.

While I made every effort to be accurate with facts and dates, and while I engaged town and village historians for much assistance, I accept all responsibility for any errors or misstatements.

Richard L. Williams
11/1/2010
Clinton, New York

Introduction

In 1947, the *Utica Observer-Dispatch* collected several columns by David H. Beetle and published *Along the Oriskany*, a 190-page book tracing the history, economy and the natural aspects of Oriskany Creek in its run to the Mohawk River. It told the story of the creek, the valley, the geography, the geology, the people, the canal and railroad, the Indians and the iron mines and blast furnaces. After sixty-four years, it's time to take a twenty-first century look at the valley and the creek to gauge changes and also constants, as they apply to the residents, farmers, sportsmen and visitors alike.

Waterways mean different things to different people. Recreation, scenic vistas, sources of drinking water, energy to run factories, irrigation and transportation of cargo represent some common uses of waterways. Shorter and smaller than rivers, creeks meander all over central New York, draining watersheds from higher elevations to rivers and lakes at lower elevations. This was all made possible by the glaciers that covered the area. The Oriskany's role has changed over the years, from one of significant economic importance (energy from water power) to municipal drinking and recreational uses. The creek made an early impact on the economy of the valley and as a source for the early settlers to find water for drinking and protein from fish.

Citizens of the valley have built dams, sluiceways and bridges to control and use the natural aspects of the creek. All of this has affected the history of the creek, its waters and the people around it. For example, drownings have occurred, and flooding has happened over the years, causing damage to buildings and roads.

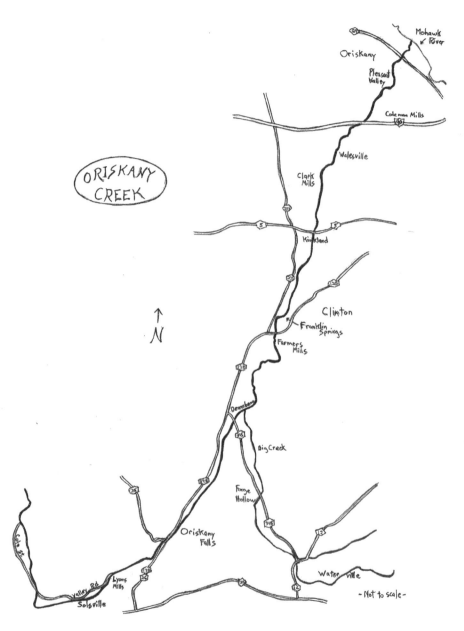

Map of Oriskany Creek. *Courtesy of Tim Pryputniewicz.*

Chapter 1

The Oriskany Creek
Watershed Changes

By Jim Cunningham,
President of the Madison County Federation of Lakes

O riskany Creek drains two watersheds crossing two county boundaries. A watershed is the area of land that contributes water to a specific body of water through streams, rivers, overland sheet flows or groundwater. A watershed may be large or small, and the term is often used interchangeably with lake basin or drainage basin. The ridges and hills that divide or direct water movement into a drainage basin define the boundaries of a watershed. Different watersheds have very different water quality, depending on soil composition and the degree of human activities.

Oriskany Creek flows northward into the Mohawk River and continues eastward where it combines with the Erie/Barge Canal. Oriskany Creek waters are augmented by waters from the old Chenango Canal system of reservoirs and canal feeders. The Oriskany Creek watershed was expanded by the construction of the Chenango Canal in the mid-1830s, which affected the water volume and quality. These waters flow through land, supporting many living organisms and human activities. We all live within watersheds of varying sizes that have a variety of human activities. The size of the watershed or drainage area affects the volume of water flowing into soils, groundwater, wetlands, creeks, streams and rivers. Human activities within a watershed contribute to soil erosion, nutrient and chemical runoff, which have a negative impact on water quality. Water, often called "the universal solvent," has a great ability to dissolve organic and inorganic materials as it moves through a watershed.

When the Chenango Canal system was constructed in the mid-1830s, the original Oriskany Creek watershed was expanded. Man-made reservoirs and canals that once flowed south were diverted and designed to flow north into the Oriskany Creek watershed. The amount of water flowing into Oriskany Creek was tremendously increased due to the Chenango Canal influence. The Chenango Canal ended its forty-two years of operation in 1878. Water, however, continues to flow directly into Oriskany Creek just north of Solsville, New York. The wooden sluice that once conveyed the canal waters over Oriskany Creek is long gone, and today, water flows from three of the Madison County reservoirs, canal feeders and streams to provide added volume and water chemistry from distant watersheds.

Historically, the Chenango Canal was completed in 1836. It facilitated transportation from Binghamton to Utica and connected the Susquehanna River to the Erie Canal. It was the first reservoir feeder canal design in the United States, and seven lakes, ponds and reservoirs were developed into what is referred to as the southern feeder system. Eaton Brook Reservoir; Hatch Lake, Bradley Brook, Lebanon and Lake Moraine Reservoirs; and Woodman and Leland Ponds all fed the summit or high point for the Chenango Canal.

College Street's three-arch stone bridge, Clinton, circa 1950. It was removed 1960. *Courtesy of Clinton Historical Society.*

Geology, History and People

Waters from the Eaton Brook Reservoir were combined with the southerly flowing water of Calahan Brook (running through the Village of Morrisville), combined with waters of the Eaton Brook watershed and the Chenango River and flowed to a splitter (any device to break up water flow into different directions) just south of Eaton. The combined waters remain split today, flowing down both the Chenango River and the Chenango feeder with gates that are managed by the New York State Canal Corporation. The Chenango feeder flows south toward Randallsville and then flows back north along the village of Hamilton's western foothills. The Chenango feeder enters the Chenango Canal near Woodman Pond and continues past Bouckville, where it passes under U.S. Route 20 just before it enters Oriskany Creek north of Solsville.

Hatch Lake and Bradley Brook Reservoirs also feed the Chenango feeder canal system. Kingsley Brook Reservoir, now called Lebanon Reservoir, was designed to feed waters through the Kingsley Brook feeder to the Chenango Canal. The Kingsley Brook feeder is still intact and still owned by the state but is no longer used.

Madison Brook Reservoir, now called Lake Moraine, discharges into Payne Brook, which flows through the Village of Hamilton and then into the Chenango River. Just below the Lake Moraine dam is a canal splitter that allows water to be diverted into the Madison Brook feeder, flowing west to the south end of Woodman Pond and ultimately into the Chenango Canal system. The canal corporation manages this splitter to divert the reservoir's water as needed into the Chenango Canal and ultimately into the Erie/Barge Canal. Woodman Pond became a water supply source for the village of Hamilton until the village developed its own wells. Woodman Pond is no longer used to feed the canal system.

Leland's Pond, now called Leland Pond, feeds into a stream flowing a short distance to the Chenango Canal. The old Leland Pond feeder, flowing south to enter at the southern end of Woodsman Pond, is still owned by the state but is no longer used.

Currently, only Eaton Brook, Lake Moraine and Leland Pond, three of the seven water sources that were the southern feeder system, continue to be managed by the canal corporation, directing waters to flow north into Oriskany Creek. Their combined flow and their respective watershed drainages collect and deliver nearly twice the volume of the original Oriskany Creek, where the Chenango Canal mixes with Oriskany Creek just south of Solsville.

HUMAN IMPACTS ON ORISKANY CREEK'S WATER QUALITY

The impact of the mid-1800s Chenango Canal is still evident today in the added water volume it supplies to Oriskany Creek and the water quality composition from its exposure to the land and human activities in these distant watersheds. These feeders collect water flowing through communities and thousands of acres of agricultural land, including wastewater discharges. The reservoirs supply cold water that is discharged through valves and pipes beneath the dams, pulling water from the bottom of the reservoirs, where water temperatures average fifty-five degrees even during hot midsummer months. The cold water is beneficial to coldwater fish species, such as trout, that thrive in the canal feeder streams downstream from the reservoirs. All the reservoirs today have a wide range of aquatic plant, fish and herbivore species, including many nuisance invasive species. All the reservoirs that today feed water into canals and into Oriskany Creek have state-operated public boat launches that allow the introduction of invasive species as boats move from lake to lake. Invasive aquatic plants, fish and herbivores exit the reservoirs and flow down the feeder canals into Oriskany Creek. For example, the canal waters are laden with both floating and submerged algae and cause the feeders to look like green soup in the summer months. Further evidence of the impact of the mid-1800s drainage alteration from the distant watersheds can be found in flood frequency and the introduction of agricultural nutrients into Oriskany Creek.

The canal corporation operates and maintains the system, under the New York State Thruway Authority's budget and control. The New York State Department of Environmental Conservation (NYSDEC) recently imposed new stringent regulations requiring evaluations, monitoring and a high level of maintenance of the reservoir dams, which are over 166 years old. The miles of feeders are filling with fallen trees and vegetation, often blocking emergency overflows. It is uncertain what will happen to the reservoirs and canals in the future due to the increasing cost of maintaining the NYSDEC-designated high-hazard dams, the miles of feeders and the many structures showing signs of degradation. Time, economics and local political support will play an important role in how long the system remains intact and flowing into Oriskany Creek.

Oriskany Creek would have lower stream flows without the added flow from the southern canal feeder system and the Chenango Canal. A natural-flowing stream is defined by its high- and low-flowing water variations. Oriskany Creek's path will change over time as a result of less flow and

Chenango Canal covered with aquatic life, between Solsville and Bouckville, 2010. *Courtesy of Jim Cunningham.*

smaller peak flows if the Chenango Canal ceases to flow into the creek. A decrease in invasive species, nutrients and chemicals could occur if the canal system was abandoned and Oriskany Creek returned to its original natural watershed condition. Three of the current eight wastewater treatment facilities would no longer enter Oriskany Creek. The Covidien Health Care industrial manufacturing facility in Oriskany Falls, which will close by the end of 2011, will eliminate another wastewater discharge point, leaving four wastewater sites discharging into Oriskany Creek.

Oriskany Creek can swell and overflow its banks rapidly. The soils beneath Oriskany Creek have a significant geological composition of limestone and deep beds of subsurface gravel that allows water to soak in and recharge the groundwater aquifer. When snowmelt occurs during spring thaws, the Oriskany Creek aquifer becomes saturated and cannot absorb more precipitation, often resulting in severe flooding. The soluble limestone deposits beneath Oriskany Creek are beneficial to the stream's biology, as they act as a pH buffer and are an excellent alkalinity (capacity of a water to neutralize acids) source. Precipitation in the watershed has been measured for its level of acidity over the years by the laboratory staff at the Clinton Wastewater treatment facility, and the watershed was found to have an acidic pH, ranging from 3 to 4 (acid rain). During the same period, Oriskany Creek water has been measured and found to maintain a pH of 7 to 8, which is advantageous to a healthy fishery and microinvertebrate population. This neutral pH value helps increase successful natural spawning of trout in the creek, thus allowing NYSDEC to stop stocking trout.

The creek was upgraded by NYSDEC from a BT (bathing and trout) classification to a BTS (bathing, trout and spawning) classification in the mid-1980s. There are eight wastewater treatment facilities that are permitted to discharge into the Oriskany Creek watershed and the Chenango Canal system, which flows into Oriskany Creek. All of the treatment facilities have been upgraded to secondary biological treatment, and some are designed to meet tertiary treatment standards, providing a high level of treatment for biochemical oxygen demand, total suspended solids, nitrogen and fecal coliforms. This advancement in treatment technologies is a result of the 1972 Federal Clean Water Act and subsequent funding. This has improved Oriskany Creek water quality, supporting the higher level of water quality required for a BTS classification.

A number of human activities in the Oriskany Creek watershed have the potential to affect water quality negatively if not managed properly. There

Chenango Canal pours into Oriskany Creek, south of Solsville, 2010. *Courtesy of Jim Cunningham.*

are currently three golf courses in the watershed that apply tons of fertilizers, herbicides and pesticides to their grounds. It would be nice if these chemicals would stay on the golf course surface, but severe wet weather flushes these chemicals into the watershed groundwater and streams.

The overall watershed supports a vibrant agricultural community. Agricultural nonpoint (pollution from land runoff or drainage) sources have the potential to increase nutrients in the Oriskany Creek watershed if not appropriately managed. NYSDEC, Agriculture and Markets and County Soil and Water Conservation Districts all help to manage large farms under a recently developed Concentrated Animal Feeding Operations (CAFO) program. There are a large number of CAFO farms within the Oriskany Creek and Chenango Canal watersheds.

One of the most important interactions between human activities and the Oriskany Creek watershed is the human consumption of its waters. Many communities along Oriskany Creek enjoy the excellent water quality that the aquifers provide. Most municipal wells are very close to the creek and are less than sixty feet deep. Although the gravel aquifers provide sufficient filtration for particulate matter, natural filtration will not provide protection against various dissolved chemicals that could enter the watershed and seep into the aquifer.

A water splitter. Water on the left goes to the Chenango Canal; water on right goes south to the Chenango River, below Eaton, 2010. *Courtesy of Jim Cunningham.*

As communities and industry developed, Oriskany Creek received millions of gallons of untreated municipal and industrial wastewater. It was not until the mid-1950s that communities were required to provide minimal solids-settling or primary wastewater treatment. Twenty years later, secondary biological treatment was required by the 1972 Federal Clean Water Act to reduce biodegradable pollutants. Most of the Oriskany Creek wastewater facilities currently provide advanced nutrient removals that, combined with the recent CAFO management requirements, have had a positive effect on the water quality of Oriskany Creek. The economic growth of the Oriskany Creek watershed that began in the mid-1800s—including the construction of the Chenango Canal and resulting human exposure to additional watersheds—changed the natural watershed for nearly two centuries. In the future, the economics of the Oriskany Creek communities may not expand as rapidly as in the past, but water quality may benefit.

Author's note: With this introductory chapter, Mr. Cunningham has aptly explained the role of the seven artificial Madison Lakes and how they provided water for the summit of the Chenango Canal. Some of them continue 175 years later to supply a water flow through Oriskany Creek to the Erie Canal. The impact of various nutrients and chemicals on the Oriskany's water quality was also described. The creek and its tributaries come next to gain an overview of the geography and setting.

Chapter 2

The Stream, Creek, the Falls and Its Tributaries

The Oriskany Valley looks, in a way, like a Y on a topographical map, as it consists of two large creeks that merge at Deansboro. The Oriskany's west branch starts near Cole Street around 1,500 feet above sea level in the Town of Stockbridge, while Waterville or Big Creek begins around 1,940 feet above sea level on Tassel Hill in the Town of Marshall. The Oriskany pours into the Mohawk River just north of the Village of Oriskany at 410 feet above sea level.

In the twenty-three miles from Tassel Hill and twenty-six miles from the rolling hills of Stockbridge, the steady and constant drop in the creek provided the first settlers with the necessary energy to harness the water power with the technology of the early 1800s. The Oriskany really turned the wheels of commerce and industry prior to the electrical age, which started in the 1900 period for most communities along the creek and its tributaries. Oriskany Creek commands the attention, respect and usefulness of the land, and people who have come into contact with it in two ways: the good—energy and recreation—and the not so good—drowning, floods and pollution.

The creek provided water power for all sorts of industrial uses, such as gristmills, sawmills, cotton factories and trip hammer shops. Dams and sluiceways to capture and direct the waters were common, and some can still be seen. The creek was a key energy source during most of the nineteenth century, and some years in the twentieth century, farmers pulled water for irrigation of their crops.

Turkey Falls on Turkey Creek in the Town of Marshall. *Courtesy of Clinton Historical Society.*

The creek clearly dominated the early economy and history of the Oriskany Valley, but since the electrical age in the early 1900s, the commercial uses have fallen way off. Its aquifer is a source of drinking water for Oriskany Falls and Clinton. The creek is used for outflows from wastewater treatment plants in Oriskany, Clark Mills, Clinton and Oriskany Falls. Today, and for many years, the Oriskany has captured the attention of fishermen as it is one of the best brown trout streams in New York State.

The western branch of the Oriskany starts as a trickle some $2\frac{3}{4}$ miles southeast of Munnsville and about $2\frac{1}{2}$ miles north of Solsville near Cole Street. Big Creek actually has two eastern branches that begin on Tassel Hill in the Town of Marshall. One branch parallels Canning Factory Road, also known as Tassel Hill Road, goes west and joins the other branch just north of Main Street and west of State Route 315 in Waterville.

The other branch of Big Creek begins about 1,600 feet above sea level in the Town of Marshall on the slopes of Tassel Hill and flows west. It parallels

Small falls in fishing access area just north of falls in Oriskany Falls. *Courtesy of Marc R. Goldberg.*

Upper White Street, to Waterville, and joins Big Creek on the west side of State Route 315 just north of Main Street. Big Creek empties into the Oriskany just north of Deansboro near California Road. Never a substantial mode of transport, Oriskany Creek today is hardly navigable depending on the water levels. From Kirkland to the Mohawk, a canoe would provide a paddler a pleasant ride, although trees and other obstructions would be a hindrance.

Numerous tributaries feed the creek in its journey to the Mohawk. In the Town of Kirkland, there are these branches: Kirkland Glen, Root Glen, Turkey and White Creeks and Sherman, St. Mary's, Gridley, Bogusville, Keyes, Miller, Munger, Eley and Martin Brooks.

Big Creek is the main branch in the Town of Marshall. Buckley Mill dumps into the creek in Oriskany Falls, and just north of Walesville, Dean's Creek, one of the longest tributaries, enters the creek.

To a traveler passing through the Oriskany Valley in 1785, the country presented all the indications of an unbroken wilderness, according to Gridley's 1874 *History of Kirkland*. The traveler's path was an Indian trail, and if he came down the hills on the west, "he looked upon a sea of forests undulating over the knolls and slopes which diversify the valley," Gridley said.

Dam just south of College Street bridge in Clinton. The water was diverted to a gristmill which burned in 1910s. *Courtesy of Clinton Historical Society.*

The Oriskany never served as a major means of travel, but in earlier times, boats were hauled upstream with cargo as best as could be done depending on the water levels. The year 1789 was called the "year of scarcity," as crops were poor. Clinton men brought the life-saving supplies home from Fort Plain via the Mohawk River and the Oriskany. They used a log canoe to pull the supplies to Clinton, a physically demanding chore using paddles, poles and ropes! The Clinton people paid for the Indian corn with ginseng, which then was gathered around Clinton.

An observer could see the Trenton hills to the north and catch an occasional glimpse of Oriskany Creek as well as the hills which rise to the east and south. The valley can best be seen from any road leading east off Skyline Drive or atop Grant Hill or Gridley-Paige Roads in the Town of Marshall. Pick any sunny fall day when the foliage peaks to observe the hills on both sides and the view north to gain an appreciation and perspective of the scope and beauty of the valley. Broken by several roads, the heavily forested hillsides and farm fields stretch out in the pleasing panorama. The west hills lead to the 1,380-feet-above-sea-level Prospect Point off Skyline Drive in the Town of Kirkland, where, today, several radio towers can be seen. Crow Hill rises to 1,303 feet on the eastern hills near Chuckery Corners.

Chapter 3

The Geology under and at the Sides of the Creek

OVERVIEW

By Donald B. Potter, Professor of Geology Emeritus Hamilton College

The bedrock formations encountered in the valley of Oriskany Creek, from its junction with the Mohawk River at Oriskany to its headwaters in the Town of Stockbridge, are part of a classic sequence of sedimentary formations exposed in central New York state. Without exception, these layers, which were deposited between 500 million years and 350 million years ago, are of marine origin. That is, they were deposited on the ocean floor at various depths and in various environments in what geologists refer to as the Paleozoic Era. Many of the formations are crowded with fossils. Three periods within the Paleozoic are represented by these formations along Oriskany Creek: Ordovician, Silurian and Devonian.

The overall arrangement, or structure, of these formations, which have an aggregate thickness of some four thousand feet in central New York, is very simple: they are stacked like a deck of cards, one above the other in regular order, with the oldest formation at the bottom. They are inclined down to the south, away from the Adirondack Mountains. Erosion over a long period of time has cut into the north edge of the stack so that we now see the oldest formation at the mouth of the Oriskany and successively higher (and younger) formations as we ascend the creek toward its source.

These formations, which have been studied by geologists since the early 1800s, form the core of a sequence extending from Albany to Buffalo and south from the Adirondacks to the Pennsylvania border. Their simple structure and their wealth of invertebrate fossils enable geologists to compare readily these formations with other similar sequences on other continents, especially those on the British Isles. In brief, they are used as a standard for understanding earth history in North America.

The early geologists named each successive formation for a locality where it was best observed. An imaginary trip up the Oriskany Valley illustrates this. The oldest formation (at the bottom of the stack), at Oriskany, is the Utica Shale of the Ordovician Period, a jet-black sequence of muddy layers rich in organic matter. Above this is the Frankfort shale, another accumulation of mud, sand and limestone, and south of Kirkland we encounter the overlying Oneida Conglomerate. This is a distinctive formation consisting of rounded pebbles of white quartz that formed as a beach deposit in the Silurian sea.

This hard rock is well exposed at Rock City, off Route 12, near Old Paris Road in the Town of New Hartford. Above the Oneida are the Sauquoit sandstones and shales and the three Clinton iron ore beds, the most distinctive layers in the entire sequence. Though not more than three to four feet thick, these red sedimentary layers consist of small pellets—the size of tapioca or BB shot—composed of the iron oxide hematite. The Clinton iron ores were mined in the vicinity of Clinton from 1797 to 1963, first as a source of iron with smelters at Kirkland and Franklin Springs and later as a source of paint pigment.

Overlying the Clinton hematite layers is the hard, durable Herkimer Sandstone, which was quarried on Brimfield Street and used as a building stone at Hamilton College. The sand grains in this rock are cemented together by the mineral dolomite, which is akin to calcite or limestone but with component of magnesium. The Lockport formation, above, is largely a hard dolomite that is well exposed in the Dugway near Farmer's Mills. When groundwater seeps through this formation, it dissolves some of the lithium, bromine and iodine, along with more common elements from the rock. This gives rise to the (now ended) Split Rock Lithia Springs bottling industry at Franklin Springs, which existed between the late 1800s and early 1970s.

Over the Lockport at the Dugway are major exposures of the Vernon shale, a thick, dull red, soft chippy rock formation that is used formerly to grade sidewalks at Hamilton College. The green Camillus shales lie above this and below the Bertie "waterlime"; it's called this because, when this dolomite is crushed and dried, one only has to add water to make it harden like cement.

Geology, History and People

The layers of the Bertie, seen at Prospect Hill and elsewhere, show abundant mud cracks that formed when the soft muddy dolomite was exposed to hot drying winds back in Silurian time, 415 million years ago. There are also conspicuous casts of salt (NaCl) crystals indicating that the seas were strongly saline. In fact, the Bertie can be traced westward to New York state's famous salt deposits known as the Salina formations near Rochester.

Above the Bertie are the Manlius and Coeymans limestones, both of which have layers loaded with fossils. The Manlius is well exposed at the crest of Prospect Hill, and both formations are seen in and near the rock quarry at Oriskany Falls. Their abundant fossils allow geologists to date the Manlius as upper Silurian and the Coeymans, as the lower Devonian. Also at the quarry at the falls in the Town of Marshall, we see the well-known Oriskany Sandstone with its fist-sized brachiopod shells. The Oriskany, only fifteen to twenty feet thick, was deposited as clean beach sand. It can be traced to southwestern New York, where it is the major reservoir rock for gas and oil.

Evidence for continuing existence of rather peaceful shallow seas during Devonian time comes from the Onondaga limestone formation above the Oriskany Sandstone. This formation is not only crowded with fossils but it holds scattered blobs of hard gray chert, a form of silica or quartz deposited on the ocean floor along with the limestone. This chert not only enhances this rock as a road-building material today, but it also must have provided Indian tribes with valuable tools for hunting and farming.

A marked change in the character of the Devonian ocean is recorded by Hamilton shales and sandstones that lie above the Onondaga limestone. No longer were the seas shallow and clean—a major continental convergence between North America and Africa was occurring in the vicinity of the Hudson Valley. Chains of mountains formed in western New England, shedding vast quantities of mud and sand into the Devonian seas in central New York. The result was deposits of the Hamilton shales, sandstones and siltstones, many layers of which are abundantly fossiliferous. They are seen in the higher ground at the headwaters of Oriskany Creek and in the hills south of Bouckville.

Thus ends the brief history of the sedimentary rock formations between 350 and 500 million years ago in the Paleozoic Era. What's happened in the last 350 million years? Three major things have taken place:

1) The Adirondack Mountains have risen to the north. This uplift or doming of the mountains was spasmodic, but it resulted in the southward tilting of all the Paleozoic sedimentary formations we have considered along the Oriskany.

2) During this long interval, a major amount of erosion by streams and rivers occurred, exposing the Paleozoic sedimentary formations discussed

above. South-trending valleys, such as those occupied today by Oriskany Creek and the Finger Lakes, were cut by streams at this time.

3) About one million years ago, global climate cooled and continental ice sheets advanced from Canada deep into continental United States.

But New York State was not overrun by the ice until late in the game, about twenty thousand years ago. At this time, an area southeast of Hudson Bay was the center of ice accumulation, and the Laurentide Ice Sheet, which flowed from there, completely overrode New York and adjacent states. It moved as far south as Long Island, where it deposited a terminal moraine, a chain of deposits that make up the backbone of the island.

Moving along at the rate of a few inches or a few feet each day, the Laurentide Ice Sheet oozed slowly into the basin of Lake Ontario and, no doubt, gouged it deeper than it had been. As it rode south over the low ground, connecting Syracuse, Rochester and Buffalo, it plastered down much of its load of mud and pebbles in the form of drumlins: long streamlined hills about one hundred feet high. There are more than one million drumlins in this field, second in size only to the great drumlin field of Ireland. Farther south, the ice funneled into dozens of south-trending stream valleys and gouged each valley deeply and smoothly into the classic Finger Lakes.

What about the Oriskany Valley?

The Laurentide Ice Sheet, perhaps over a mile thick, covered all the hills and valleys in central New York. Because it was thickest in the valleys and some of these valleys trended in the direction of ice movement, a great deal of erosion occurred there. As the nearby hills were smoothed and rounded, the Oriskany Valley was straightened and deepened. It is essentially a poor cousin to the main Finger Lake Valleys.

As the climate moderated about ten thousand years ago, the Laurentide Ice Sheet continued to flow southward, but the ice thinned, and the front or snout of the glacier retreated northward in stages. First it stood as far south as Long Island and along a curved course on the Pennsylvania border, then it withdrew to the latitude of Binghamton and then to the south ends of the Finger Lake Valleys. At each of these pausing stages, the ice and the voluminous melt waters that were coming from it deposited a moraine, which we see today as knobs, hills and ridges of sand, gravel and unsorted glacial till. The most prominent of these moraines is the Valley Heads Moraine at the south ends of the Finger Lakes and at Oriskany Falls.

The valley floor of Oriskany Creek is quite flat and deep just north of the village because it was occupied by ice. Southward, at the village, there is an abrupt three-hundred-foot rise of the land marking the snout of the ice and then a broad morainal zone of kames (small hills) interspersed with kettles. Each kettle is a deep depression formerly occupied by a stranded block of glacial ice. Voluminous meltwater deposited sand and gravel between the ice blocks, so that when the ice blocks melted, small hills (kames) of sand and gravel are seen interspersed with depressions where the ice blocks had been. Southward from this moraine, the valleys of the Chenango River and its tributaries are filled with glacial outwash (more sand and gravel) from the melting glacier. The conspicuously flat floors of these valleys make good farming terrain.

As the ice retreated northward in the Oriskany Valley, it halted once more just north of the Dugway, a place where Oriskany Creek swings to the east and cuts a narrow valley. One-half mile south of Franklin Springs there is a conspicuous flat-topped island in the middle of the valley. The irregular north slope of this island marks the snout of the wasting ice that paused here for several years in its retreat, damming the meltwaters and forming a glacial lake in the upper part of the valley. Sands and gravels washed from the wasting ice and formed a delta seen today as the flat-topped island in the middle of the valley. The glacial lake likely extended south to Deansboro.

Hanson Quarry, in the Town of Marshall, along State Route 12-B, 2010. *Courtesy of Marc R. Goldberg.*

With further wasting and thinning of the ice in the valley, meltwaters deposited sand and gravel in depressions on the surface of the ice, so that when the ice completely melted, there remained a small hill or kame, as at Christmas Knob on Norton Avenue. Farther north, near Old Bristol Road, deposition took place in crevasses in the ice, forming a short string of kames.

The limestone quarry at Oriskany Falls has been active since 1830s and now is owned by Hanson Company, which supplies colprovia and stone for roadwork and construction. Other smaller quarry operations took place in Kirkland, too. Most of the stone for Chenango Canal locks was quarried locally, although canal histories refer to the stone in the locks as "rubble stone."

SOIL

Hamilton College professor Oren Root in the 1850s described the soil as clayey loam with beds of sand and gravel. The alluvial deposits along the shores of the Oriskany are rich in fertility.

The soil is rich, producing the best of Indian corn, barley, oats and wheat. The soil is gravelly loam in valleys and clayey loam on the hills of Oriskany Valley; undulating and rolling upland, fine sand loam is also here. Soil leads to a fine place for crops such as hay and corn and wheat. Orchards and vegetable gardens abounded; hillsides are wooded with maple, beech, birch, oak, chestnut, ash and evergreen trees.

The *Utica Daily Observer* of September 7, 1850 stated, "The soil of Kirkland is rich, producing the best of Indian corn, oats, barley, and wheat. The Flatts made by Oriskany Creek are of the richest mould and its meadows will vie with the Flatts of the Genesee Valley, as to beauty or richness of soil."

Today, field crops such as corn, hay, wheat, and barley for dairy cows and soybeans, green beans and sweet corn for humans dominate.

This survey of the geology and land of the valley shows how the environment impacted the history during the past 230 years. The natural surroundings provided the water, the minerals and the seasonal climate that promoted the area and gave the residents the tools to live and prosper. Native Americans never had major villages in the Oriskany Valley, but they certainly hunted here, were involved in a Revolutionary War battle and negotiated a treaty line that sliced through the valley.

Chapter 4

Fauna and Flora

Most consider the Oriskany one of the best fly-fishing streams in upstate New York; it's particularly known for brown trout. As early as 1789, Dr. Samuel Hopkins wrote that "Orisca Creek contained plenty of trout and is surrounded by excellent lands." The state and private fish and game clubs have done much over the years to keep the Oriskany a prime stream for sportsmen.

In 1882, the Kirkland Fish Stocking & Protection Society had about $50 that was used to stock the Oriskany with carp, 30,000 brook trout, 20,000 California mountain trout and 215 German carp. A report from Colonel J.T. Watson, secretary, said the "Creek is swarming with young bass, the product of the Society's first year of stocking." The April 11, 1885 *Clinton Courier* reported that 250 German carp were placed in the Oriskany by Kirkland Fish Stocking & Protection Society, led by Colonel J.T. Watson, and that fishing was prohibited for three years. In a July 1901 stocking of the creek, 7,000 infant trout were taken out by train on New York Ontario & Western Railroad and freed at various points along the creek. The young trout came from a New York State hatchery at Randolph. In 1995, the New York State Department of Environmental Conservation released 5,100 brown trout, and normal stocking has become a normal procedure.

Unfortunately, some fish died at times. Thousands of fish died in June 1937, and in 1957, hundreds were found dead; no reasons were ever announced.

John Pitarresi, sports writer for the *Observer-Dispatch*, entered Hamilton College in Clinton in 1966 and quickly took his hobby of fishing to Oriskany Creek. We are pleased to present his reminiscences here:

I had fished for trout only once before I arrived in Clinton in 1966.

I had grown up on the Niagara River, fishing for bass and walleyes—yellow pike locally—and catching mostly sunfish and silver bass. Once, we took a trip to Wiscoy Creek way down in Wyoming County. We were 12 or so and didn't see a trout.

We've seen a lot of them on Oriskany Creek the last 45 years or so.

I discovered the creek the spring of my freshman year in college, having been all but unaware of it flowing at the base of the hill for months beforehand. My friend Mike Small, a skilled outdoorsman, asked me to go fishing with him up in the woods off Dugway Road. That's still a favorite spot of mine, as much for the scenic woods and placid surroundings as the fishing.

I remember it was a beautiful day, and I remember my first trout. I was leaning up against a hemlock tree that hung over a deep hole. I dropped my worm-baited hook in there, and a few minutes later pulled out that trout, all nine inches of him.

There have been a great many trout since, all over the state, out West, and a lot of other places, but Oriskany remains my home water.

It is a terrific home water. Few creeks filled with trout are so accessible. Close to Utica and Rome, coursing the through the villages of Oriskany Falls, Deansboro, Clinton, and Clark Mills, paralleled by good highways much of the way, the Oriskany is easy to reach. Yet, though it receives far more pressure from anglers than most streams its size, the quality of its fishing remains very high.

The Oriskany, which reportedly teemed with brook trout in Colonial times, long ago became a brown trout stream, although brookies still can be caught, especially near the mouths of its many little tributaries. And the browns tend to be very nice. You can expect to catch many trout from 9 to 14 inches in the creek, but there are much larger browns to be had. My neighbor, Ron Janowsky, a very good worm fisherman, once caught a 24-incher near the Route 5 bridge, and there are similar fish out there. Even larger now and then.

The average size of Oriskany browns has gone up considerably since the Department of Environmental Conservation began stocking 2-year-old fish about a decade ago. These fish, usually 12 to 15 inches long, provide quality fishing, and a certain number of them winter over and grow larger still. About 750 of them are stocked each year from Clark Mills upstream to Deansboro. Another 16,000 smaller fish are put in over the course of the season.

Clinton fisherman Abe Adour with his catch in 2010. *Courtesy of Charles J. Kershner/Clinton Courier.*

Not all Oriskany trout come out of a hatchery. There is a good amount of natural reproduction, especially above Deansboro, where the DEC does not stock. Those wild fish, which tend to be smaller than the trout downstream—but not always—are beautiful examples of the species. There aren't many things prettier than a wild Oriskany brown, unless it is a wild Oriskany brookie.

Catching Oriskany trout isn't necessarily easy, but you can have some big days on the creek if the fish are in the mood. There are many ways to skin a cat, but I have my own favorite methods.

Early in the season, when melting snow and rain make the creek high and muddy, I like to use spinner-and-worm and spinner-and-minnow combinations. And I've talked to some anglers who have had great success using big, noisy bass-size lures like Rat-L-Traps.

As the water clears later in April, I'll use Panther Martin spinners and small Rapalas. I like combinations of black and gold and also, believe it or not, hunter orange.

Once the mayfly and caddisfly hatches begin—sometimes early in April and for sure by the third week of the month—I use a fly rod almost exclusively. Some of the best hatches on the creek include the Hendricksons in late April, followed by Pale Evening Duns, Green Drakes, and the tiny Tricorythodes flies in August and September. Nymphs and streamers, like the Wooly Bugger, are always an option when there are no flies on the water.

No matter how you approach it, you will have a great time fishing the Oriskany. It's a gem.

The New York State Department of Environmental Conservation, in a 1990 biological assessment, stated that "no significant water quality problems [were] indicated." The stream has been upgraded and sewage and waste reduced significantly with wastewater treatment plants being built since 1980 in Clinton, Oriskany Falls, Clark Mills, Waterville and Oriskany.

Wild animals of the Oriskany Valley also listed by Oren Root in the mid-1800s were black bear, lynx, red fox, wolf, weasel, rabbit, skunk, raccoon, muskrat, red, grey, and black squirrels and woodchuck. Today, the white tail deer is prevalent, and the wild turkey has made a comeback in the past twenty years. A few snakes—nonpoisonous—exist here, along with turtles that are sometimes seen dead on the highways

The several birds identified by Root in the 1850s were owl, eagle, hawk, crow, crane, pigeon, snipe, blue jay, kingfisher, woodpeckers, robin, oriole,

Dugway Road and Oriskany Creek, circa 1930, Town of Kirkland. *Courtesy of Mel and Evelyn Edwards.*

blackbird, cow bird, yellowbird, partridge, bluebird, catbird, chip bird, hummingbird, bobolink and several sorts of thrush, wren and swallows.

In 1982, the Kirkland Bird Club participated in the annual Christmas Bird Count in southern and central sections of Oneida County. Here is its long list of birds seen: great blue heron, black duck, goshawk, Cooper's hawk, red-tailed hawk, rough-legged hawk, American kestrel, ruffed grouse, ring-necked pheasant, turkey, herring gull, mourning dove, great-horned owl, barred owl, flicker, woodpeckers (several varieties), blue jay, horned lark, crow, titmouse, chickadee, nuthatch, cedar waxwing, northern shrike, starling, myrtle warbler, sparrow (several varieties), eastern meadowlark, finches, grosbeak, redpoll, pine siskin, junco, starling, snow bunting, Lapland longspur and robin.

Animal habitat depends on forests and natural cover. Over half of the county's original forests were gone by the 1970s. In the past fifty years, with climate change and acid rain being analyzed by scientists, the habitat for wild animals could change again.

VARIETY OF TREES

Dr. Oren Root in the mid-1800s listed these trees for the Oriskany Valley: various varieties of the maple, elm, white and black ash; white and red beech; black and yellow birch; basswood; buttonwood; hornbeam; bitternut; butternut; wild poplar; wild cherry; hemlock; white pine; and, more rarely, tulip tree, white oak, larch, black spruce and white cedar.

The Reverend Samuel Kirkland planted Lombardy poplars on College Hill Road between 1804 and 1808. These had been brought from Philadelphia, where Thomas Jefferson had imported them from France. They lasted nearly one hundred years.

In Clinton between the 1850s and 1900, the Rural Art Society planted several trees not native here. The gingko tree in the parking lot of the Dollar General store is an example of this. American elms, which lined streets throughout the Oriskany Valley, were mostly lost to Dutch elm disease in the 1950s. Another tree of note still grows since circa 1810 on the north side of College Street at Oriskany Creek in the Town of Kirkland. This is a buttonwood or sycamore tree, which was planted by property owner Clark Wood. A 120-foot-tall Norway spruce was declared the tallest in New York state in 1996; it grows 4 feet to 8 feet a year in Root Glen at Hamilton College.

All along the Oriskany Valley, there are glens that have added beauty and a diversity of plants to the area. An article in the March 30, 1892 *Clinton Courier* said that

> *not one of them is more picturesque than Kirkland Glen, now called Root Glen. The brook has some delicious secrets it has never told to many, and not a few tiny trout may exist in the shaded pools. Blackberries grow in abundance and thimbleberries, too, opened their great white blossoms wooing bees on the steepest bluffs. It is a glen of rare beauty.*

Today, New York has more forest land area (62 percent) than it had 150 years ago due to widespread abandonment of farms.

While the natural world of the Oriskany and Big Creek Valley has been shaped by glaciers and waterways, animals, plants and weather, the inhabitants also have made an important impact on the valley, too. How the settlers and citizens lived and made a living, how the region developed economically and how all this changed through the years will be detailed in the histories of the several hamlets and villages.

The environment of the Oriskany Valley provided the setting and the natural characteristics for the residents, who took what they found and adapted it to their uses. Now, what happened to the previous wilderness after Europeans arrived in the 1790s will be discussed.

Chapter 5

Indians of the Creek and Valley

The Oneida Indians

The Iroquois Confederacy occupied much of the land in today's New York state from the 1100s through the arrival of the Dutch and English settlers in the 1600s and into the 1800s, when Indian land was taken by the state at several treaty occasions. The Five Nations (Seneca, Cayuga, Onondaga, Oneida and Mohawk) became the Six Nations when they adopted a displaced North Carolina tribe, the Tuscaroras, in the early 1700s.

The Oneidas were a matrilineal society with the women cultivating the maize and the men, the warriors, hunting and fighting when necessary. Clan mothers held power and elected chiefs. The Oneidas split with other Iroquois and fought with the colonists during the Revolutionary War along with the Tuscaroras. The Mohawks were firmly in the British camp mainly due to Sir William Johnson's influence.

New York state leaders made outright grabs of Indian lands after the war at various treaty signings, many at Fort Stanwix in today's Rome. New York governor George Clinton was an unabashed land speculator with partner George Washington, and Clinton used his position to acquire thousands of acres of land and extinguish Indian land rights throughout the state. Many of these efforts were in direct conflict with the federal Non-Intercourse Law that required federal oversight and agreement for Indian lands to be transferred.

Some scholars maintain that the state's policies were designed to clear the Indian title so turnpikes, canals and eventually railroads could cross New

York state. A quick look at a map will show that Oneida and other Indian land lie directly in the path of these public works ventures. As a result of Clinton's aggressive land acquisition policy, the Oneidas were reduced to a reservation of thirty-two acres near Munnsville.

The Oneida settlement in colonial times was at Oneida Castle, some ten miles west of Kirkland and Marshall on the Seneca Turnpike. Also at "Oriske," or "Oriska," the Oneidas had a village where Oriskany Creek flows into the Mohawk River.

One missionary attending to the Indians was the Reverend Samuel Kirkland, who came from Connecticut in the 1760s and spent the rest of his life here in an attempt to take the Gospel and white men's ways to the Indians. Kirkland built a house on Harding Road in the Town of Kirkland, which survives though much enlarged. The Oneidas and New York state

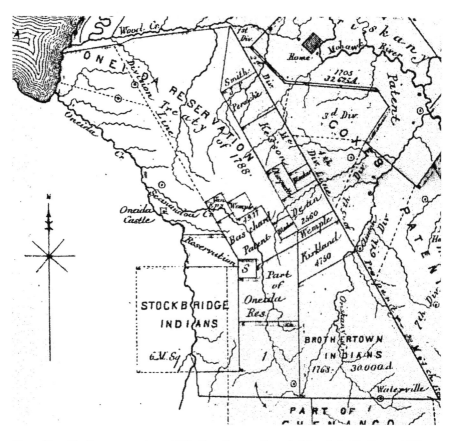

Map of local Indian reservations, 1829. *From Surveyor General's Map of Oneida County, 1829.*

granted Kirkland over four thousand acres in 1788. Kirkland developed his plan to educate Indian youth and started the Hamilton-Oneida Academy in 1794 on three hundred acres of land he donated. In 1812, his academy was chartered as Hamilton College, now nearing its 200th anniversary.

Both James Dean and Samuel Kirkland were Indian interpreters at various land treaties here, and both received land grants. Back then, land was money, and the poorly paid missionaries sold off their donated lands to make ends meet. Some critics have questioned this arrangement and wonder about the exact motivation of Dean, Kirkland and other missionaries. Similar to the plight of the Brothertown Indians, many Oneidas moved to Wisconsin, also starting in the 1830s, and settled near the Brothertowns.

However, in the late 1980s, the Oneidas, led by nation representative Ray Halbritter, have purchased many acres of former Oneida land and now operate a casino, bingo hall, golf courses, farms, gas stations and other businesses. This Indian prosperity has since caused many political battles with lawsuits and clear divisions of opinion. The Oneidas refuse to pay taxes on land they have bought and refuse to collect state sales taxes on sales to non-Indians despite court decisions sustaining the government's position. In 2010, an agreement to allow vendors at the casino to pay taxes was finalized. In 2011, the U.S. Supreme Court agreed to hear one of the Oneidas' cases.

THE BROTHERTOWN INDIANS

In colonial Connecticut, many pressures for Indian land by white colonists, plus King Phillips War and disease, decimated various tribes by the mid-1700s. Parts of different tribes gathered to live around Farmington, Connecticut, where there were many Tunxis Indians. Some Indian leaders developed a plan to move remnants of several tribes away from that area to start anew.

The Indian leaders wrote letters to Mohegan, Niantics, Groton Pequots, Stonington Pequots of Connecticut, Narragansetts of Rhode Island and Montauks of Long Island urging migration.

Representatives went to central New York and the Oneida Indians, who granted the Brothertown Indians land in today's Oneida County towns of Marshall and Kirkland, some ten to fifteen miles southwest of Utica. This was in 1773, but the Revolutionary War halted more migration plans, as some who had migrated returned to New England, and some spent the war at Fort Stanwix in today's Rome.

Leaders of the Brothertown Indians were the Reverend Samson Occom (1723–1792), a Mohegan who was an ordained Presbyterian minister; David Fowler, a Montauk; and the Reverend Joseph Johnson, a Baptist minister and a Mohegan.

Samson Occom had a whimsical side, too, which is seen in this letter to his two daughters when he was in England:

> *"My dear Mary and Elizabeth,*
> *Perhaps you may query whether I am well. I came from home well, was*
> *by the way well, got over well, am received at London well, and am treated*
> *extremely well…yes I am caressed too well. And do you pray that I may be*
> *well and that I may do well, and in time return home well. And I hope you*
> *are well, and wish you well, and I think you began well, so keep on well,*
> *that you may end well, and all will be well.*
> *And so farewell,*
> *Samson Occom*

In the 1784 period, about 200 English-speaking Brothertown Indians settled and began a community of farmers who practiced Christianity. The Oneidas and New York state gave the Brothertowns land of twelve by thirteen miles but reduced it to two by three miles in 1788 in the Treaty of Stanwix. About 450 Indians lived there at its peak. New York state reduced the grant in 1796 to nine thousand acres, and the state sold off 149 lots to whites who were anxious for the rich land.

Quaker missionary Reverend John Dean arrived in 1795 and started a school and a church. His son, Thomas Dean, became the Indian agent after his father died, and Deansville was named after him. It became Deansboro in 1894, as U.S. mail often went to Dansville, New York, south of Rochester in confusion. Thomas Dean actively sought land in the Midwest for the Brothertowns, as white settlers yearned passionately for their acreage. Many Indians leased or sold their land to whites even though that was not supposed to happen.

Due to white encroachment and their insatiable thirst for land, Brothertowns were besieged to lease and sell the land given them by New York state and Oneida Indians by the 1830s. Many Brothertowns traveled to Wisconsin and settled on the east side of Lake Winnebago in today's Calumet County. However, in 1839, the federal government ended their status as a recognized tribe and made all the Brothertowns U.S. citizens, and the reservation was sold off. In Wisconsin, many intermarried with European immigrants, such as the Swedes, Norwegians, etc., and easily assimilated into Midwest culture.

Most Brothertowns had left Oneida County by the 1880s, but a few remained and died here. There are two Brothertown cemeteries in the area, and some are buried in the Deansboro Cemetery just north of Deansboro. The last of the Brothertowns here was Romance Wyatt, who died in 1908 and was buried in the Deansboro Cemetery.

Unfortunately, for the remnants of the seven or eight New England and Long Island tribes, the Brothertown plan did not work. This was due to a combination of poor leadership, religious and political divisions and white encroachment. Additionally, a lack of industry caused by the people's affinity for alcohol doomed the venture from the start.

Today, a small hamlet sign of "Brothertown," a couple of historic markers, a Brothertown Road and two old burial grounds are about all that remain here of the experiment to preach Christianity, to civilize and to assimilate these Indians into white man's ways and mores.

Over three thousand Brothertown Indians are officially enrolled today, as the tribe now seeks to be recognized again by the federal government. However, after several years of petitioning and waiting in August 2009, the application for recognition was denied.

The Brothertowns are now appealing and currently maintain an office in Fond du Lac, Wisconsin. They still do not have their own land, but they do have a governance structure, have elections for leaders, do Indian arts and crafts and meet socially in other cities of the Midwest. A bingo committee holds weekly games in the Spectrum in Fond du Lac to raise funds to help in the appeal. The tribe's financial situation is quite limited; it owns no land and has requested its enrolled members to make donations.

In 2011, the Brothertown Indian Nation maintains a website at http://www.brothertownindians.org. Richard Schaderwald was the chairperson in 2010 and directed the activities of the Brothertowns, which included bingo, federal recognition, annual homecoming, a quarterly newsletter, monthly council meetings, sales of craft items and tribe history. The Brothertowns dream of owning tribal land some day and are raising funds to meet their goal.

THE STOCKBRIDGE INDIANS

Although not the main focus of the Oriskany watershed, the Stockbridge Indians of Munnsville occupied a part of the Town of Stockbridge near one source of the creek. The Stockbridge Indians came from the Housatonic Valley in Massachusetts in 1785 to land given them by the Oneida Indians in today's Town of Stockbridge, Madison County. The Reverend John Sergeant was their spiritual leader as his father had been when the tribe was in Massachusetts.

The pattern of white encroachment on rich timber lands happened to the Stockbridge Indians, too, and in the 1830s, they moved to Wisconsin. Originally on land near Kaukauna, the federal government enticed them to move to Lake Winnebago in Calumet County. This is where Oneidas and Brothertowns also settled. In 1856, the Stockbridge-Munsees moved again to Shawano County and have a reservation of 22,139 acres today.

The tribe merged with the Munsees and has gained federal recognition as the Stockbridge-Munsee Band of Mohicans. Today, about 1,500 members are enrolled Stockbridge-Munsee Indians, and 900 live on the reservation.

In November 2010, the Stockbridge-Munsees of Wisconsin signed an agreement with New York governor David Paterson to relinquish land claims to 122 acres in the town of Stockbridge. The Indians will retain 1.84 acres for a public park. In exchange, the state agreed to allow the Stockbridge-Munsees to go ahead with a casino/resort in Sullivan County in the Catskills. This could take time, as several legal hurdles could block the way. The New York Oneida Indians oppose the agreement, and said they'd take the agreement to court. In February 2011, the U.S. Department of the Interior denied this casino plan of the Stockbridge-Munsees.

The original inhabitants of the Oriskany and Big Creek Valley in the colonial period were systematically moved aside through numerous treaties to clear the way for white settlers to move in and farm the productive land. Once the Indians moved west, they were not an element in the development of the valley. Currently and since the 1980s, the Oneida Indians have established a major commercial presence in the Turning Stone Casino and have bought hundreds of acres of land in both Madison and Oneida Counties.

Chapter 6

Military History

About two miles west of where Oriskany Creek enters the Mohawk River, one of the bloodiest battles of the Revolutionary War took place on August 6, 1777. As part of the New York campaign, Lieutenant Colonel Barry St. Leger, with a combination of Loyalist forces and Mohawk and Seneca Indians, moved from Oswego to capture Fort Stanwix in today's Rome. Then he could meet up with Generals John Burgoyne and Sir William Howe in Albany, thus splitting New York and the colonies in two. The plan nearly worked, but the siege failed after Indian allies fled following the bloody encounter at Oriskany.

St. Leger led about 660 British, Loyalist and Canadian forces, a Hanau Jager detachment and 500 of Sir John Johnson's King's Royal Regiment of New York, plus about 1,000 Mohawk and Seneca Indians.

General Nicholas Herkimer had 750 men of the Tyron County Militia, mostly poorly trained German American farmers, and some 60 Oneida and Tuscarora Indians. They marched from German Flatts and Herkimer's Home with the Tyron County Militia in August to raise the siege. Never reaching Fort Stanwix, Herkimer's long train of ox carts and wagons was ambushed by Mohawk chief Joseph Brant (1742–1807) in a small valley (ravine). This was about two miles west of where Oriskany Creek empties into the Mohawk River near the Indian Village called Oriska. Hand-to-hand combat ensued, and blood ran freely.

General Herkimer was mortally wounded in the first volley of the concealed attack, but he calmly directed his forces while smoking his pipe and propping himself up on his saddle by a beech tree. A violent thunderstorm on a hot afternoon interrupted the battle for a few hours. At about 2:00 p.m., the garrison from Fort Stanwix led by Colonel Marinus Willett sortied out and sacked the British and Indian camp, capturing or destroying numerous military stores and supplies. The Indian forces led by the Senecas withdrew, and the British plans to divide the colonies failed.

About 450 Patriots were killed, wounded or captured, while the Indians and Loyalists had 150 dead and wounded. This battle split the Iroquois, as Mohawks and Senecas fought for the British, while Oneidas and Tuscaroras were with the colonists. While Herkimer did not reach Fort Stanwix, St. Leger was unable to meet in Albany with Howe or Burgoyne to split the colonies as planned. The battle cost the Patriots dearly, as Herkimer suffered mortal wounds and was taken by barge down the Mohawk to his home where his leg was amputated. He died on August 16 due to an inexperienced attending doctor and poor medical procedures.

The battlefield site remained in private hands until the Oneida Historical Society (now the Oneida County Historical Society) acquired a small parcel of land on which to build the obelisk. A grand and gigantic celebration occurred on the centennial of the battle of August 6, 1877 in daylong

Oriskany Battlefield, August 1777, Town of Whitestown. *Courtesy of Mel and Evelyn Edwards.*

ceremonies and speeches. About eighty thousand were estimated to have attended on foot, horseback, wagons and carriages, boats, steamers and rail. An "imposing military and civic parade" took place. In 1884, the then new obelisk monument was dedicated. The battlefield is now a state historic site under a joint management agreement with the National Park Service.

The Old Moyer Road deserves brief mention in this military section. The old local history texts say that early Kirkland/Clinton pioneers followed what was known as the "Old Moyer Road," which brought them to Paris Hill and, turning north thence, to the present site of Clinton. This was an old Indian trail from the Mohawk River to Oneida Lake and on to Buffalo.

Ada Marie Peck, writing in 1901, related how the "Old Moyer Road" had been the subject of much discussion. It was believed by early settlers, she went on, to have been named for General Moyer, who passed over it to fight Indians. However, no General Moyer existed.

Others have maintained that a series of logs in corduroy-road style were found near Paris Hill and other places along the road. Peck also gave a date, April 19, 1779, when fifty-five men under Colonel Goose Van Schaick passed over the road from Fort Schuyler to burn the Onondaga Indian village south of today's Syracuse. Peck also stated that General John Sullivan, with a large body of men, passed over the road in September 1779. The 1995 *Tour of Hanover* stated that Sullivan's army encamped on land at Oriskany Creek just west of today's Lumbard Road and felled timber to build a bridge over the Oriskany, as it was too deep to ford. Also, the Reverend J.W. Wicks maintained that Sullivan's army cut logs to pass over a swamp east of Paris Hill.

So, what can be made of the Moyer Road story? The direct route for Van Schaick from Fort Stanwix in Rome to the Onondaga village would not have passed along Moyer Road. It would have been shorter to travel over the land west of Rome to Syracuse along the later Seneca Turnpike, which originally was an Indian trail. However, the "Moyer Road" name did stick around in local history writings. In an April 5, 1855 mortgage foreclosure legal notice of the property of Eli Hull, the name Moyer Road was used in the legal notice.

The road came from Mohawk or Ilion to Paris Hill and then west along today's Maxwell Road, passing McConnell's Corners at Post Street and then named Barker Road from Barker's Corners to Lumbard Road, previously called Whitney's Corners. Today, no evidence of Moyer Road exists across Oriskany Creek until State Route 12-B at Bogusville Hill Road. Old histories say an Iroquois log home of two rooms once stood on the east side of the creek there in the "Indian Lot."

In summary, no evidence supports Moyer Road being a route of the Sullivan or Van Schaick troops. However, the name has lingered and was used in the 1800s.

The Battle of Oriskany disrupted many Mohawk Valley families, but the Oriskany Valley had not been settled yet, so a lasting impact did not occur. The major result of the battle was to clear the area of British troops, except for some raids later during the Revolutionary War such as at Cherry Valley.

Chapter 7

The Upper Reaches of the Valley

Prior to the first permanent settlements here in the 1780s, white men had explored and missionaries had attempted to convert the Indians. Jesuit missionaries Isaac Jogues, Rene Goupil and Guillaume Coutaure were brought here in 1641 by the Mohawks as prisoners of war. They had time to explore the Mohawk Valley, but in 1700, all Jesuit priests were expelled from New York. Then, various Protestant missionaries such as Samuel Kirkland in the 1760s visited the local Iroquois.

English traders followed Dutch ones to profit from the lucrative beaver fur trade. The Ice Age had left the Mohawk River and its tributaries, such as the Oriskany, a rich and beautiful area stretching from Albany westward for one hundred miles. Today it's a short two-hour drive, but in the colonial days, it could have taken a man on a horse two days or a settler a month walking next to an ox cart.

THE LAND

Originally used as hunting and fishing grounds by the Oneida Indians, the Oriskany Valley watershed in New York's colonial period was divided between the colonists and the Iroquois at the 1768 Fort Stanwix Treaty. This treaty line runs from Fort Stanwix in today's Rome southeast through Oneida County on its journey to the Susquehanna and then west. It crossed College Hill Road in Clinton just west of State Route 233. East of the line,

Oriskany Creek. *Courtesy of Clinton Historical Society.*

the colonial governors had granted land patents to favorite politicians and families. This colonial land policy failed to stem the tide of white settlers.

Land grants were called patents. The Coxe Patent covered parts of the Oriskany Valley, as did the Brothertown, Wemple, Otsequette, Kirkland, Dean's, Bleecker, Oriskany and McKesson Patents. West of the Fort Stanwix Treaty Line of 1768 was Iroquois land. Some of these patents were given by the Oneida Indians jointly with New York state (Kirkland, Dean and Wemple) and were west of the 1768 treaty line.

Dean and Kirkland came here as missionaries and interpreters and received the land as a reward from grateful Indians. Wemple was an officer in the Colonial army, and he was awarded land for his service. After the Revolutionary War, early New York politicians like Governor George Clinton and General George Washington bought over six thousand acres of land in parts of the former Coxe Patent, as speculators and made out pretty well. In fact, some of the land holdings of Washington were not sold to settlers until after his death on December 14, 1799.

Land speculators quickly developed plots of land for sale, and hordes of New England residents migrated into the Oriskany Valley towns and hamlets. Peter Smith will be discussed later, but he was an example of a land baron who became rich from land sales. After the Revolutionary War in 1784, the Oriskany Valley was in Montgomery County until 1791, when Herkimer County was formed. Oneida County was taken from Herkimer in 1798, and the valley—except for the creek's western branches, which originate in Madison County—lies mostly within Oneida County.

The "Yankee Invasion" was aptly named for the movement of former Revolutionary War soldiers and their families coming to the Oriskany Valley to farm and start new settlements. The desire for land, depletion of New England soil and dislike of special privileges of the Congregational church caused much of this migration.

James W. Darlington wrote in an October 2003 *New York History* article that these early settlers more often than not set the cultural tone of a place, one that remains clearly evident long after the early settlers have left the scene. This flood of basically self-sufficient settlers brought values of hard work and religion of the staunch Calvinist variety. Early churches were organized in the 1790s to spread the Gospel and provide a central place to worship and hold social events. As one example, the Society of Clinton started in 1791 and today is the Stone Presbyterian Church. While New England Yankees were among the largest regional group, the New York frontier attracted settlers from all of the northeastern states and several foreign countries, a study for some other historian to undertake.

TOWN OF SANGERFIELD

The Town of Sangerfield, the county's southern-most town, was started in 1792 by Colonel Jedediah Sanger (1751–1829), who owned much of the land and built a sawmill. Sanger also founded the Town of New Hartford and became a prominent entrepreneur in the area, a judge, New Hartford town supervisor and a state legislator.

The Town of Sangerfield was surveyed in 1789 and in 1791, and it was formed from the Town of Paris in Herkimer County on March 5, 1795, consisting of 19,188 acres. It was the twentieth town of the Chenango Twenty Towns land, and in 1797, the Town of Bridgewater was taken off. The Town of Sangerfield was transferred to Chenango County in 1798 and then to Oneida County in 1804.

David Norton became the first supervisor from 1795 to 1800, and Thomas Brown, the first town clerk. Justus Tower was the next supervisor from 1803 to 1804, while Erastus Jeffers served from 1834 to 1836. Norton was a militia colonel, and Sanger was justice of the peace and postmaster.

Several communities are in the Town of Sangerfield, including Sangerfield Center, Stockwell, Pleasant Valley and the Village of Waterville. Geography played a big role in the development of this area just north of Sangerfield Center, as there was a divide between the Mohawk River and the Chenango River. A stream was found that flowed north to the Mohawk River and was named Big Creek. This provided much of the water power for shops and factories, as the creek drops four hundred feet between Waterville, or the "Huddle," and Deansboro alone. The population moved north about one mile to house the laborers, mill rights and other workers; this small community—today's Waterville—was originally called the Huddle. The Chenango River is just over the divide from Big Creek and drains through the Nine Mile Swamp south of the Cherry Valley Turnpike, eventually joining the Susquehanna River in Binghamton, New York.

Note that Kate Loftus Welch, who taught in the Forge Hollow stone school, wrote columns for the *Waterville Times* in the 1920s and 1930s and entitled them Along Willona Creek. That term never caught on. It's Big Creek today.

A private stock company continued to build the Cherry Valley Turnpike in 1803 from Cherry Valley to Manlius, and four- and six-horse stages became common vehicles. The state chartered the Third Great Turnpike Company and allowed it to collect tolls every ten miles. The private firm abandoned the venture in 1859. At Sangerfield Center, the Cherry Valley Turnpike caused commerce to increase in the 1810–1811 period. All animals, sheep, cows, hogs and turkeys were driven to market in Albany. A "cattle drive" meant the animals walked, accompanied by drovers.

Three men were instrumental in early Sangerfield history, as they were the town's original owners: Judge Sanger, Michael Myers and John J. Morgan. Sangerfield Center was the center of population at first as the Cherry Valley Turnpike came through. Commerce followed the drovers with their cattle and sheep, and inns sparked rural prosperity.

What to name the new town? Many had chosen "New Lisbon," but Colonel Sanger stepped in, promised a cask of rum for the first town meeting and conveyed twenty-five acres to the Congregational Society and twenty-five acres to the Baptist Society if Sangerfield was the choice. It was.

The "Lisbon" Congregational Society in Sangerfield began in October 1796. It built a church in 1804 on the green, which is now lost to a wider turnpike. This was the only church ever in Sangerfield Center, and it eventually served as the town hall until it was demolished in 1961. Now the Town of Sangerfield's highway barn occupies that land.

At Sangerfield Center, with Colonel John Williams as the first postmaster, the post office can be traced from 1808. It moved to different buildings through the years. In 1993, it was in a former garage, and in 2011, it now shares the town offices in the Sangerfield Municipal Hall. Mail came weekly via horseback and then stage coaches in the early period. After the rails arrived in 1868 and until 1940, mail came that way. Now trucks bring the bills and the magazines.

The 1907 atlas map shows the Sangerfield Brick and Tile Company on the turnpike, the DL&W tracks, the town hall, a one-room school and the Sangerfield Cemetery, which is still active, on State Route 12 just north of Route 20.

The Cherry Valley Turnpike (National and State Route 20) was paved in 1920–1923 and was enlarged to four lanes in the 1939–1940 years. Route 20 is the longest federal highway, going from Newton, Massachusetts, to Newport, Oregon. This road was named the "Empire State Turnpike" in 1925.

At Sangerfield Center in 2011, the commercial activity has Michael's Restaurant, Nice 'n Easy, a gas station, Oneida Asphalt Company, Curtis Lumber, Titan Homes, Blue Seal Richer Feed and FSGrownmark. Set just off Route 20 is the World War II monument that lists fifteen Sangerfield veterans who lost their lives in the war.

Sangerfield-Richer Feeds, along State Route 20, 2010. *Courtesy of Marc R. Goldberg.*

Another hamlet in the Town of Sangerfield is Stockwell, east of State Route 12 where, in 1907, a Methodist church and a school operated. Stockwell had three sawmills, one cheese factory, a cider mill, a gristmill, a blacksmith shop, a hotel and a store in 1871. The former Stockwell church and school went to Americana Village near Lake Morraine just north of Hamilton in the 1950s.

Pleasant Valley west on the Cherry Valley Turnpike now has a Grange Hall and a greenhouse and garden center. It had a one-room school one hundred years ago. Often called "Christian Hollow" years ago, a sawmill operated in the 1820s. Farmers used a level mile-long stretch of Route 20 to test their horses in "scrub" races.

Village of Waterville

In his 1878 *History of Oneida County*, Samuel W. Durant says that Nathan Gurney was the first settler in the Huddle in 1793, the year Sanger built a sawmill. Benjamin White had a gristmill in 1795. Sylvan Dyer kept a tavern and ran a store in 1799, thus beginning the mercantile base of the Huddle, today's Waterville. By the 1830s, Waterville had one thousand residents, along with gristmills, breweries, tanneries and iron foundries—all dependent on Big Creek for power.

Hops, an additive for beer and ale, came to Oneida County and the Waterville farm community in the 1820s; most villages had a brewery in the early days. In Latin *Humulus lupulus*, hops dominated the Waterville/Sangerfield economy positively into the 1920s, bringing wealth, new homes and mansions, along with a vibrant social and cultural life to the area.

The arrival of the railroad in 1867 gave hop farmers a better means to move the crop to market. Waterville was the Hop Capital of the World between then and 1900, but competition from western states caused hops to peter out in the area, although some farmers tried to keep hop yards into the 1920s and some even later.

Waterville was a leader in changing the hop industry with innovations such as the hop stove, hop press, hop picker and hop extract. One hop business was the Waterville Hop Extract Company (1875–1935), which had a plant on today's State Route 315. Twenty thousand pounds of hops a day were processed. The extract was the first extract of uniform quality available, and it was shipped around the country. Hop prices in area farms were a fluctuating source of extra income for the farmers, as the market prices went up some years and down the others. From twelve to fourteen

Mill Street, circa 1880 (now State Route 315), in Waterville. This is a view north toward Forge Hollow. *Courtesy of Waterville Historical Society.*

cents a pound in the mid-1860s to fifty to fifty-five cents a pound in 1883, hop prices dropped dramatically to six cents a pound in 1895.

Fifteen to twenty hop merchants and agents played big roles in the economy, and hop extract was made and shipped from the village. After the peak in the 1900 period, hops declined due to diseases, insect and "blue mold," soil depletion, less tolerance for alcohol, the emergence of the more reliable dairy industry and competition from Oregon and Washington state growers. Additionally, some breweries changed ingredients for beer. Farms could ship raw milk by rail, which also caused farmers to cease raising hops because it was an unreliable cash crop. Farm income from hops was 57 percent and 37 percent from dairy in 1900. Twenty-five years earlier, it was 81 percent hops and 16 percent from dairy operations. Prohibition of the 1920s also was a death knell in the Waterville hop economy. In 1930, seventeen acres produced only eight thousand pounds of hops, a mere fraction from the heydays of the 1880s.

A hop renewal of sorts took place in the World War II period with International Grain Company and John I. Haas Brewing Company.

Ye Olde American Hotel on East Main Street, Waterville, circa 1950. *Courtesy of Richard L. Williams.*

They raised hops again, using the latest machine techniques for growing, harvesting and drying hops. By 1944, instead of 17 acres, 375 acres were under cultivation, producing 190,000 pounds of hops. This experiment in bringing back hops quickly faded away as a victim of high labor costs, poor variety production and overhead expenses. The big firms pulled out, and the hop culture and economy in Waterville ended. Dairying and cash crops such as beans, potatoes, green beans, squash, broccoli, sweet corn, soy beans and peas became the mainstay of the local farmers. Simply stated, milk replaced hops.

Victorian mansions on Putnam Street were built with hop money. Many show the architecture of the Victorian period. Italian Villa–style homes with nearly flat roofs and one with a cupola, plus lots of roof bracketing, were typical of the period. One mansard-roof home is also located on Putnam Street.

A fine example of this wealth in buildings was the Waterville Opera House, which went from Main Street to White Street, next to Ye Olde American Hotel and across from the former Waterville Presbyterian Church. The opera house was built in 1880 and hosted numerous social and cultural events through the years. In the post–World War II period, it held the Strand Theater, and now it stands empty and unused. The Ye Olde American Hotel was demolished by the bank in March 1964, allowing a new bank to be constructed on the triangular lot at White and Main Streets. This hotel had been a Loomis Gang hangout in the mid-1800s and is credited to builder Jonathan Hubbard in 1814. About 150 years of history vanished with the hotel's demolition.

Community pride also surfaced in the period when hops were king of the town and of the economy. On June 10, 1899, to commemorate service in the Civil War by Waterville and Sangerfield veterans, the Grand Army of the Republic (GAR) erected a monument on the triangular area called Monument Park, where Route 12 swings south. The bronze eight-foot-high Civil War soldier was added in November 1904. To honor later veterans, the granite monument and freedom light were dedicated on July 4, 1969, to veterans of the Spanish-American War, World Wars I and II, the Korean War and the Vietnam War. In the summer of 2010, a new Victorian-style bandstand was placed in the adjacent village park. The new bandstand is a memorial to those who created the village and community.

In 1794, a serious accident happened when a settler had his left leg badly broken when it was crushed by a falling tree. He was taken to the home of a Mr. Hale in Sangerfield on a Saturday. A surgeon was needed quickly, so Hale rode the only horse in town by the light of a torch and arrived the next morning in Whitestown. Failing to find a surgeon Hale rode to Fort Schuyler (Utica), where he found Dr. Gatineau, who returned with him. Dr. Petrie of Herkimer was also procured to assist, and on Tuesday, the leg was finally amputated. Today, two medical offices and several dentists take care of local residents.

Monument Park, Waterville, circa 1900. *Courtesy of Waterville Historical Society.*

Another indication of life on the frontier is this will abstract from the book of wills in the surrogate's court for Oneida County for the years from 1814 to 1823.

Wightman, Stephen, Esq. of Sangerfield, weak in body but sound of mind. Leaves wife Margaret Wightman, mare and colt, side saddle and bridle, linens, and clothing, 50 good apple trees. Oldest son, Amasa Wightman, sole executor, to receive $80 out of estate of Robert Patrick, his grandfather on mother's side. Also was a bequest to Wealthy Loomis. Remainder of estate, real and personal, to be divided equally among children: daughters Lucinda, Achsah, and Lovina and sons Amasa, Ira, Eber, and Patrick. 4 people witnessed the will which Wightman signed with his mark. Will made 6 May 1813.

A post office began as early as 1796 in the Huddle in a tavern owned by Colonel Amos Muzzy, who was the first postmaster. In 1808, the Sangerfield post office was moved to the Huddle but returned to Sangerfield Center on the Cherry Valley Turnpike. It wasn't until 1823 that the post office went back to the Huddle along Big Creek. The site of Waterville's post office moved through the years to different buildings on Main Street; it opened in 1961 at 101 West Main Street. Honoring Corporal John P. Sigsbee, twenty-one, who was killed in Afghanistan in January 2008, the post office was renamed the Corporal John P. Sigsbee Post Office on January 16, 2009.

By 1808, the Huddle was named Waterville at a meeting in a tavern. Names that were rejected included "Whisky Hollow" and "Whiskeyville"; they were suggested due to a number of distilleries operating. Dr. Sherman Bartholomew suggested Waterville, and the post office was changed to that in 1823. About two hundred people lived there then in thirty-two homes. Early commerce developed in the Huddle, with a tannery employing seventy to eighty hands and a Cold Springs Brewery on Mill Street. Amos Osborn ran a distillery between 1802 and 1815; in 1860, a blind and sash mill was operated by A.B. Cady and Son; J.A. Berrell had a foundry and machine shop that began in 1837; and three hotels were in existence in the 1815 period: Ye Olde American Hotel of Jonathan Hubbard, the Park House and the Commercial House.

Waterville village residents voted to incorporate on February 8, 1871, and David B. Goodwin was first president of village, with Henry J. Coggeshall as the first clerk. The village marked its centennial in August 1971 with appropriate celebrations, including a centennial ball and weeklong events such as a parade, dances, fireworks, walking tours and old-time entertainment. Proceeds from the celebration were used to microfilm all copies of the *Waterville Times* to preserve them for research.

Newspapers came early to the Sangerfield area, starting with the *Civil and Religious Intelligencer* in 1815. It became the *Sangerfield Intelligencer* and *Madison and Oneida Counties Gleaner* in 1830. In the 1880s, the *Waterville Reflex* was printed. The *Waterville Times* began in 1856, and it is published weekly now by Pat Louise from 128 East Main Street. She bought it from Mary Cleary in May 2001. In 1963, W. Douglas Sexton ran the paper, having bought it from the Westcott Estate. William W. Jannone took over in 1972, and Mary C. Cleary purchased it in April 1979. It covers the southern Oneida County area and is the official newspaper of most local governments.

A driving park off Sanger Avenue (State Route 12) from 1886 to the 1910 period gave horses and drivers a nice oval for trotting and harness racing. A mare called Flora Temple was born to a sire that belonged to the Loomis family near Waterville in 1845. She was later owned by a Dutchess County man who saw the mare's racing potential and entered her in many races around the country, from Maine to Michigan and Louisiana to Long Island.

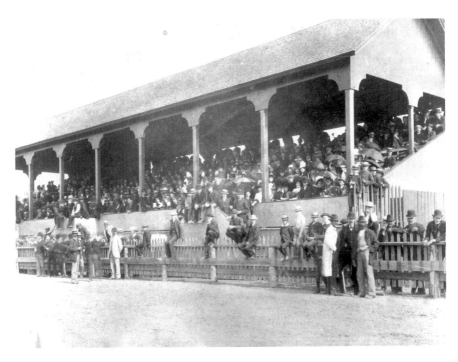

Driving Park, Waterville, circa 1900. *Courtesy of Waterville Historical Society.*

A subject of Currier & Ives lithographs, Flora Temple was the first trotter to break a 2:20 mile. Flora Temple was so popular that several babies were named after her. She died on December 21, 1877.

Hotel Waterville had the first liquor license after Prohibition ended in 1933. Mrs. Anna Alsheimer Small operated the hotel between 1927 and 1973. When it was built in the 1830s, every brick was wrapped and brought from Europe. Today it is called the Red Lion Pub.

Other restaurants in 2011 are The Huddle on Main, La Petit Maison and the Village Diner. No fast-food chains have landed in Waterville yet! Two banks serve customers today: First Niagara at 129 West Main Street and Access Federal Credit Union at 120 East Main Street. Main Street has other shops and stores typical of small communities.

Waterville Knitting Mill made underwear, sweaters and sportswear; it closed in 1989. Hanna Manufacturing Corporation made large portrait cameras, electronic camera parts, photographic chemicals and also rope products until it closed in 1989. The owner was Edward Hanna, who was mayor of Utica two different times in the 1990s. Other factories were Barclay Knitting Company, which closed in 1991, and the Haxton Canning Factory, which closed in 1964.

Feed stores existed to supply farmers with cattle food. Allied Mills and two Agways operated in the 1970s until 2000. One Agway in Sangerfield started in 1969, and the one on State Route 315 sold propane gas and gasoline. Now Suburban Propane operates out of that building. The Agways are both gone, as the firm went bankrupt. A local feed mill, Louis Gale and Sons, founded in 1950, still serves the farming sector and is run by Edward Gale. It is in the former Haxton canning factory and now makes cow feed from soybeans and corn. Blue Seal Richer Feeds and Sangerfield Grains have plants in Sangerfield on State Route 20, so farmers still have a choice of feed stores and plants from which to purchase feed for their herds and seed to plant.

The Utica, Chenango & Susqehanna Valley Railroad came in 1867, bringing a new era of modern transportation for passengers and farm and factory products alike. The firm sold $2,500,000 in stock for the eighty-four mile road. Daniel B. Goodwin was vice-president, and Lewis Lawrence was president. The first Waterville train station was in a three-story brick structure one hundred by forty feet, called Putnam Hall, built in 1867 by George Putnam on Putnam Street. This was later C. Buell & Son Boot & Shoe Manufacturers until 1903 and then the Oneida Hosiery Company, which merged into the Oneida Regal Textile Company in 1911; it soon closed because of financial problems.

DLW Railroad station, Waterville, circa 1900. *Courtesy of Mel and Evelyn Edwards.*

Waterville Knitting Company used the building between 1918 and 1956, making underwear, beachwear, sweaters and sportswear. Richard Pauker and his father, Michael Pauker, bought the mill in 1956 and expanded with a new plant, which was put up by Barclay Sportswear in 1970 on Conger Avenue. Michael Pauker was chairman of Barclay. However, it closed in 1992. The old Putnam Hall, used and occupied for nearly 140 years by different firms, was razed in 2007.

The UC&SV Railroad was leased as a part of the Delaware, Lackawanna and Western system in 1870, and freight trains still run today as part of the New York, Susquehanna and Western Railroad. In 1886, a new train depot, eighty by thirty feet, opened and was used for years. The last passenger train left the village in 1950.

Three plank roads went through Waterville during the plank road era of 1849 to the 1870s. One came through Clinton and Deansboro from Utica, one from Waterville to Utica through Paris Hill and another from Waterville to Earlville on the east side of the swamp. Toll houses were spaced every three miles.

The Loomis Gang, a colorful and notorious family of criminals, settled in the Nine Mile Swamp just south of Sangerfield Center after George Washington Loomis Sr. rode into the area in 1802. Loomis made his money stealing horses, and in 1806, he paid Hervey Prentice $1,700 in cash for 115 acres in lot number 10 of the twentieth township for land on the western edge of the swamp. Although accused of arson, horse stealing and counterfeiting, plus other offenses, the Loomis brothers—Wash, Grove and Plumb—never were punished by the law. However, the public's patience wore out, and in 1865, Town of Brookfield constable (some sources say sheriff) James L. Filkins led a raid on the Loomis home, resulting in Wash's death. About seven months later, a second raid looted and burned the house. Plumb Loomis was hanged almost to the point of death, but he survived and lived until 1903. Books have been written and much folklore has surrounded the Loomis family, as legends of ghosts in the swamp linger today.

Religion played a role in Sangerfield and Waterville, as seven churches organized and built houses of worship: Congregational in 1795, First Baptist in 1808–1811, Presbyterian in 1823, Methodist in 1835, Grace Episcopal in 1842, St. Bernard's Roman Catholic in 1850 and Welsh Congregational in 1851. The former Presbyterian church now houses the Southgate Ministries at 127 East Main Street.

In the early part of the twentieth century, Waterville was a lively business community with these firms: an electric light and power company, a foundry, two black smith shops, Waterville Tanning & Japaning Company, DL&W Railroad station and freight house, Borden Condensed Milk Company, coal yard, two warehouses, YMCA, library, hop merchant George W. Bishopp, National Bank, Kirkland Canning Company, Waterville Opera House, Oneida Hosiery Company and the Ye Olde American Hotel.

To provide fire and emergency protection, as early as 1829, the Waterville Fire Department began, and it now houses its apparatus in a recent new building at 222 East Main Street, which shares space for a substation with the Oneida County Sheriff's Office.

A brick school was built in 1814 on the corner of South Stafford and White Streets, and a larger one was opened there in 1872 as a Union Free School and Academy. Over the years, several one-room schools spread around the rural areas of Sangerfield, and at the time of consolidation, fifteen small common school districts decided to combine into Waterville Central School in 1928. The new district completed a school on Stafford Avenue North (State Route 12) in 1930, which cost $350,000; it is now Schoolhouse Apartments. Eastman Kodak founder and Waterville native George Eastman gave $50,000 for the auditorium as a gift. A new grades seven through twelve open-space junior-senior high school on Madison

Street opened in 1974. The Memorial Park Elementary School on East Bacon Street was constructed in 1960. Neighboring Oriskany Falls merged with Waterville in 1983, as had Deansboro in 1931.

The Tower family came to Waterville around 1802. They were from Hingham, Massachusetts. Justus Tower built a gristmill and a home, but unfortunately, he drowned in a "freshet" from Big Creek in April 1804. Reuben Tower became successful and wealthy and built the Tower Mansion on Tower Avenue. As a state legislator, he worked hard to push the Chenango Canal through the legislature, but he died prior to the canal being built.

The Reuben Tower mansion, which dates from the 1815–1820 period, is now owned by the Harding family. The Harding Nursing Home is on land to the rear of the mansion. Reuben's son, Charlemagne Tower I, had attended Harvard and practiced law in Waterville. In his later years, he became interested in mining and was a pioneer in open-pit mining. The Tower farm land and barns housed blooded horses and prize cattle. His son, Charlemagne

Tower II, became a U.S. ambassador to some European nations in the 1900 period, and Geoffrey Tower, son of Charlemagne II, was the last family owner of the mansion.

The Tower mansion housed numerous antiques, paintings and Staffordshire plates depicting the landing of Lafayette. The Tower furnishings reflected the taste and wealth of the family. One wing had French wallpaper designed about 1812 showing the Bay of Naples.

The eccentric bachelor and wealthy industrialist Reuben Tower II (1829–1900), son of the first Reuben Tower, was the last of eight children to Reuben

Reuben Tower Mansion, Waterville, circa 1910. It is now the Masonic Temple. *Courtesy of Richard L. Williams.*

and Deborah Taylor Pearce Tower. He built the Tower building in 1890 at 111 Sanger Avenue, now used by the Sanger Masonic Lodge and Crystal Eastern Star Chapter. The Masons bought it in 1940 and have continued the tradition of ringing the nine bells and Westminster chimes. The bells were rung first on July 4, 1891. The Clinton H. Meneely Bell Company of Troy, New York, cast the bells. The Seth Thomas clock became the village clock, too. The historic building was listed on the National Register of Historic Places in 1978. The Reuben Tower/Sanger Masonic building has a walk-around cupola and high windows so strollers could not see in. A wine cellar was a feature, along with the fine paneling and high ceilings. The 103-foot three-stage tower has unique features and arrangements of the bells, including a Masonic bell.

Tower II had an interesting life, being born into wealth and standing in the community. He attended Oxford Academy and Harvard University, where illness forced him to end his studies in his sophomore year. At age twenty-one, he returned to Waterville and manufactured alcohol and raised cattle, gathering a fortune of $23,500 by age twenty-five around 1855. He devoted his life to agricultural pursuits. His love for animals caused him to breed thoroughbred horses and livestock and maintain a successful farming operation with fine fields and barns. At one point, he had thirty blooded horses described as beauties that combined speed and blood.

His love for his community caused him to become both village president and town supervisor in the 1880s and 1890s. At one point, Tower was also president of the Sangerfield Driving Park. He built a waterworks on the Barrett farm in 1887 and piped the water to the Tower farm.

Tower's barns suffered a major fire on September 13, 1885. The main barn, horse barn, piggery, hay barn and two sheds burned, along with forty-one animals that included thirty-five sheep, two pigs and four calves, totaling a $20,000 loss. At that time prior to Tower building his Sanger Avenue home, he lived over the barn in a twenty- by twenty-foot room. He escaped from the blaze.

While the Town of Sangerfield supervisor in 1889, he entertained the entire Oneida County Board of Supervisors at his home, now the Masonic Temple. The *Utica Daily Observer* of June 28, 1889, had an account of the day when the board took the DL&W train to Waterville. The article detailed the furnishings in the Tower home, which included an "immense" Turkish rug, clocks, sideboards, expensive paintings, oak wainscoting and mirrors. Sixty plates were "laid" for the repast, and Professor Lombard's orchestra "discounted sweet music." The supervisors toasted Reuben with a rare sherry

Sangerfield Curtis Lumber, State Route 12, 2010. *Courtesy of Marc R. Goldberg.*

as "our genial, hearty, and noble host." Reuben Tower died on August 31, 1899, of apoplexy at age seventy and was buried in the Waterville Cemetery. The newspapers called him the "best known and most respected citizen."

The Sanger Mansion at 7124 Sanger Hill Road dates from 1906 and was finished in 1913. Colonel William Cary Sanger (1853–1921) built it, but after fifty years, the English Manor–style estate was sold to Edward W. Jones in 1954. Jones sold it to the Stigmatine Fathers in 1960. Colonel Sanger was a graduate of Harvard and an attorney. He also received a bachelor of laws degree from Columbia Law School and was a trustee of Hamilton College. Mr. Sanger had a long association with the army and the government and was a special escort to President Woodrow Wilson in 1917. He also had the distinction of being an usher at Wilson's funeral. His wife was Mary Ethel Cleveland Dodge, and she bore him four children.

The Stigmatines trained novitiates at the mansion to become Roman Catholic priests. The order was formed in November 1816 by Saint Gaspar Betoni in Verona, Italy. By 1905, the order had some members in Waltham, Massachusetts, and in 2011, it has facilities in White Plains, New York; California; and Massachusetts.

After the Stigmatines, Mr. and Mrs. John Hall bought the mansion and lived there between 1970 and 1987, when John McCormack of Connecticut became the new owner. He never lived there, and the bank held it due to a mortgage default until it sold to Dr. Stephanie O'Callaghan in 1991 as a retreat and conference center. Mark and Kathryn McLane assumed ownership of the neglected and vandalized property in 2006, restoring and renovating it. It was sold again in 2009.

The mansion is at an elevation of 1,483 feet above sea level and looks west to the Village of Madison and east to the Village of Waterville and the Tassel Hill area. It is located on 62 acres with 10,500 square feet of living space and has twenty-one bedrooms, twelve bathrooms, eleven fireplaces and a total of fifty-two rooms. The Olmsted brothers, who designed Central Park in New York City, designed the grounds, and Newton Phelps Stokes was engaged as the architect. Thirty to forty men labored to build it over a seven-year period. The stone was quarried in Oxford, New York.

Champion Homes, now Titan Homes, a builder of manufactured housing, opened a large plant on State Route 12 South in 1973 and had about 170 workers. The plant suffered a major fire in January 1999, but it was rebuilt and reopened in September 1999 with 200 employees; it remains

Sangerfield Titan Homes, State Route 12, 2010. *Courtesy of Marc R. Goldberg.*

in full operation in 2011. The firm continued to pay its employees during the nine months of rebuilding and received much praise for that action. Wickes Building Supply started a store in 1960, followed by Webb and Son. In 2011, Curtis Lumber occupies that area south of Sangerfield Center on State Route 12.

C&H Plastics began by Ray Clark and William Humphrey Sr. on State Route 315 in 1970 in the former Waterville Foundry building. C&H makes plastic molds and custom plastic thermo injections. It moved to the former Barclay Sportswear plant at 145 Conger Avenue and now occupies the fifty-five-thousand-square-foot facility. Now, pizza shells are made in the former C&H plant on State Route 315.

Two active and important community organizations are the Waterville Historical Society and the Waterville Library. The historical society moved in early 2010 from the former Welsh Congregational Church on White Street to the former Waterville Library on 220 East Main Street, which was the Brainard home. The Waterville Library, since May 2006, has a new eight-thousand-square-foot building on White Street, replacing the two-thousand-square-foot Brainard home. It serves as a social and cultural center for the village and recently has had solar panels installed.

Another indication of Waterville's architecture and history was confirmed by the state and federal governments with the listing of the Waterville Triangle Historic District on the National Register of Historic Places in 1978. This includes parts of White Street, East Main Street, Babbott Avenue and South Stafford Avenue. However, the village lost another landmark when the former Waterville public school on South Stafford Avenue and White Street was razed in 1998. This brick school dated back to 1872, and in the 1930s, it was a knitting mill. It housed the Waterville Historical Society in the early 1970s. For unknown reasons, the Qatari ambassador to Turkey, Hassan Ali Al-Nimah, bought the empty structure in 1995 and sold it to the village three years later.

Community renewal came to the village in the first decade of the twenty-first century with a new village hall in 2002 and parking for the police and residents where the old school stood. The state redid Main Street with new curbing and pavement in 2005–2010, which included some new sidewalks, decorative red brick paving, granite curbing, Victorian street lamps and a town clock, purchased by the Waterville Rotary Club, at Main and White Streets. New sewer lines also helped the environment and helped clean up Big Creek. A wastewater treatment plant went online in 1970 off State Route 315.

Durant wrote these flattering words about Waterville in his 1878 *Oneida County History*: "Waterville is growing both in wealth and population and presents a fine appearance as fine an appearance to the visitor as any village in the County. Many elegant residences bring an air of refinement and culture throughout."

Waterville is still changing, according to the *Cornell University Bulletin* of December 1954, and this could apply to many villages today:

> *the rapid means of communication and transportation evolved in the past quarter century (1954 back to ca. 1930) now make this community a part of a larger expanding region. It is subjected to new forces penetrating from the outside world and must adapt to this world. Yet it is within the village community that the primary interests of the residents will find their expression and satisfaction. The activities and associations that its organizations and institutions make possible are, therefore, vital to personal needs and hopes, and essential if society's ideas are to be sustained.*

TOWN OF MADISON

The Town of Madison was set off from the Town of Hamilton on February 6, 1807, and it is one of five towns erected in the year following the formation of Madison County. It lies in the south central part of Madison County, closely following the line of the abandoned Chenango Canal, which had stations at Solsville and Bouckville. The town contains 40.895 square miles.

The Town of Madison was lot number 3 of the Chenango Twenty Towns on land ceded to the state in 1788 by the Oneida Indians. It was named after President James Madison and contains the divide between the Mohawk and Chenango River watersheds.

The first town meeting for Madison was held March 3, 1807, with Erastus Cleveland as the first supervisor for 1807–1808. Erastus Cleveland merits some attention here, as he came from Norwich, Connecticut, and more immediately from Whitestown, while on a prospecting tour in 1792. He moved a mile below Solsville on Oriskany Creek, later called Tyler's Mills, which is where Water Street turns off Valley Road. A dam here covered several acres. Frank Fisk took over Tyler's Mills around 1885 and sold feed and ground grain for farmers. Fisk also installed a dynamo, one of four between Solsville and Oriskany Falls, making his mill and home equipped with electricity in the early 1900s. This mill site was gone by 1950.

Cleveland also engaged in buying ashes, making black salts and was a carpenter by trade. An early history said that this spot selected by Cleveland "possessed elements which the genius and energy of Cleveland made a source of wealth." Cleveland also was involved in a brewery and a distillery in Madison. General Erastus Cleveland operated six mills, a distillery, a brewery, a carding machine, cloth factory, gristmills and saw mills—all using power of Oriskany Creek. Ever the entrepreneur, Cleveland owned stock in and helped construct the Cherry Valley Turnpike, serving as one of its directors for many years.

Turning to politics, Cleveland served in the state assembly, helping pass the law authorizing the Chenango Canal; was a county judge; and promoted the establishment of a county poorhouse. He had command of a regiment during the War of 1812 at Sackett's Harbor, New York, on Lake Ontario. He was known afterward as General Cleveland; he was buried in the Madison Village Cemetery.

The Town of Madison was one of the foremost hop growing areas of the county in the late nineteenth century, and farming continues today, mainly dairy and field crops for cattle. Windmills for electricity generation appeared on the Madison landscape in 2000, and several operate in 2011, providing income to land owners.

Madison Village started in 1801 by John Berry, and it became a market and rest stop with many taverns along the Cherry Valley Turnpike, which began in 1803–1811. The village was incorporated April 17, 1816, and has the only cobblestone octagonal house ever built in the United States.

The Chenango Canal first went through Solsville in 1836. This was a 172-foot rise in the six miles from Oriskany Falls to Solsville toward the canal summit at Bouckville. In 1868–1869, the Utica Clinton & Binghamton Railroad came to Solsville. The Town of Madison bonded for $100,000 to aid in constructing it through Madison. This was a common practice then for towns to bond to get a railroad to come.

From the late 1890s to 1930s at Madison Lake, a quarter of a mile from the hamlet and near the line of the New York Ontario and Western Railroad, there were two summer hotels kept by D.W. Leland and White & Lewis. Grove W. Hinman operated the resort in the 1920s and 1930s. In a May 1922 ad announcing the opening of the lake for the summer, it described the place as having a large dancing pavilion 120 feet by 40 feet, bowling alleys, ball grounds and "ample provisions for picnic parties"—"No mosquitoes at Madison Lake." The Leland Hotel and the Lewis House, plus ten cottages, were advertised. Radio music, a six-piece orchestra, band

Madison Lake resort, 1930s, Town of Madison. *Courtesy of Madison Historical Society.*

concerts, boating, bathing and pike, bass and trout fishing were activities listed in the advertisement. This beautiful spot had many attractions for those seeking rest and recreation and attained considerable popularity in the early twentieth century. Geologically, Madison Lake is a kettle lake at 1,135 feet above sea level. The Town of Madison has run a swimming beach there the last forty or so years, and a few homes are on the west side of the lake.

HAMLET OF SOLSVILLE

James Smith wrote about Solsville in the *History of Chenango and Madison Counties*, saying, "It was once a thriving, enterprising place, but the abandonment of the canal, and the opening of the railroad have materially affected its interests."

Solsville in the Town of Madison is the first hamlet Oriskany Creek touches, although the creek actually begins north of Solsville in the Town of Stockbridge. Mainly rural with dairy farms, Stockbridge is 31.7 square miles and was formed from Vernon and Augusta in 1836. Solsville had 315 inhabitants living in 138 households in 2000. It's named after Solomon Alcott, a potash maker. Former names were Dallrymple's Mills and Howard's Mills. Solsville lies at 1,125 feet above sea level.

Solsville Mill Pond, circa 1920. *Courtesy of Madison Historical Society.*

Solsville, in 1875, had a barber shop, a cheese factory, a gristmill, blacksmith shop, store and post office, a school house, a harness shop, a canal and a railroad station—probably at the peak of its golden era. L.M. Fisher ran a gristmill below the village in 1899, and L.D. Lewis had a general store. T.B. Manchester was a blacksmith, Newton Livermore ran the hotel and the Mutual Milk & Cream Company collected milk to make cheese.

The hotel, probably the oldest business in Solsville, had a second-floor ballroom and was a busy place during the canal and railroad era—even today as well. The *Waterville Times* advertised the hotel in 1863 with S.M. Palmer as owner and boasted a new second-floor ballroom that was forty by sixty feet. R. Bridge ran the hotel in 1875. In the period after World War II, it was called Frenchy's Hotel, featuring "good home cooking" and all legal beverages. In 1955, Eva Lovett owned it, and in 1966, John and Juanita Schumaker had the license to sell beer and cider.

The *Waterville Times* advertised in 1979 that Mother's Day delicious dinners at the Solsville Hotel featured roast duck for $6.95, roast lamb for $6.95 and prime rib for $8.95. Salad bar and cherry cheesecake were included. Phil King in 1992 sold to Brad Dixon, who still operates the hotel. The restaurant is called Irish Pub at Hotel Solsville. Around the corner in 2011 is Just Another Bar.

Train tragedies occurred at Solsville in 1893 and 1927. Four hop pickers from Oswego in September 1893 tried to jump aboard a New York

Solsville Hotel, Just Another Bar and Oriskany Creek Bridge, 2010. The view is toward the northwest. *Courtesy of Marc R. Goldberg.*

Ontario & Western train moving about six to seven miles an hour. One William Farrell slipped and fell, and his head was cut off as if with a knife, according to an article in the September 5, 1893 *Utica Weekly Herald.* A truck, carrying a load of pea pickers, struck a gasoline-electric train at Fiske Crossing near Solsville in July 1927. The pea pickers were returning to a shack where they were staying in Solsville in a thunder and lightning rain storm. Four Utica pea pickers were killed, along with four critically and sixteen "painfully injured."

Borden Condensed Milk Company started the milk plant in Solsville, but later the Mutual Milk and Cream Company shipped five thousand pounds of milk daily via railroad. Dairymen's League operated the plant in the 1920s, but it burned. Grove Hinman and P. Anderson rebuilt it and leased it to a Jetter in 1922. Dairymen's League bought it in 1941, but it burned again. It was rebuilt, but the plant has been closed for several years now. The Solsville pond was the source for ice for the milk plant in the early twentieth century.

The feed mill had various owners, too. The Hard brothers from Eaton built the mill in 1910 and lived in it. After it burned in 1941, it was rebuilt by

Former Solsville Agway store, 2010. *Courtesy of Marc R. Goldberg.*

Lyon's Mill dam, Valley Road, Town of Madison, 2009. *Courtesy of Marc R. Goldberg.*

Moses Cronk, then sold to the Grange League Federation and finally taken over by Agway, which went bankrupt in 2002.

The abandonment of the Chenango Canal (1878) and the opening (1870) and then the closing of the railroad (1957) seriously affected the economic prospects of Solsville.

Solsville today is a sleepy hamlet with homes, a hotel, and some farms. The canal, the railroad, most businesses and people are gone. The community depended on a transportation technology that has been replaced by cars and trucks, and the farm sector has declined throughout the county, diminishing the rural economy. The mills are long gone, and the tracks have been torn up, but the old dam still holds back some of the creek water prior to going under the bridge on the way to Oriskany Falls.

Downstream one mile from Solsville is Lyon's Mills and a sixty-acre pond. A sawmill turned out enough wood to build three hundred homes a year and was owned by Warren Lyons between the 1920s and 1940s. Elevation at the east end of the dam is 1,100 feet.

TOWN OF AUGUSTA

The Town of Augusta partly borders the Town of Marshall on the east; the southern border is at Madison County/Town of Madison line, and the Town of Vernon touches Augusta on the north. The Town of Augusta was named after General Augustus Van Horn. Colonel Thomas Cassety promised Van Horn that if he could get a town named after him, he would give the colonel a new military hat. Cassety got the hat. The town's first settler came in 1794, and Andrew McMillan came in 1798 from North Conway, New Hampshire. After that, Oriskany Falls and Augusta began to grow, as many early settlers came from Litchfield, Connecticut.

The Town of Augusta formed in 1798 and includes 27 square miles of land. Land was leased for twenty-one years from Oneida Indians by Peter Smith—a total of 60,000 acres. Some 16,763 acres of it was on the Peter Smith Tract in the Town of Augusta. In 1795–1797, the New York State legislature said leasees could buy the land patents for $3.53 an acre.

Peter was the wealthy businessman and trading partner of John Jacob Astor. Smith's son became abolitionist Gerrit Smith, who graduated from Hamilton College in Clinton in 1818 and went on to become a staunch advocate for the blacks. He started a farm colony for them in Lake Placid (Town of North Elba) called Timbuctoo prior to the Civil War, served in Congress and was active in the temperance movement.

Cassety Hollow historical marker on State Route 12-B, Oriskany Falls, 2010. The view is south. *Courtesy of Marc R. Goldberg.*

The most prominent native-born son from Augusta was John Jay Knox (1828–1892), a financier who served as U.S. comptroller of the currency between 1872 and1884. He graduated from Hamilton College in 1849 and worked in banking prior to his government service. Another native son made his mark in the professional baseball world. Karl Spooner pitched for the 1954 Brooklyn Dodgers and appeared in two games of that year's World Series. An injury ended his brief stint in the Major Leagues.

Augusta also claimed a Revolutionary War soldier Amos Parker (1762–1842), who was with Marquis de LaFayette at Yorktown and purportedly saved his life in a close combat engagement. Parker was supposedly the tallest man in the army; however, no one has his accurate height. One source said he was eight feet tall. On Marquis de LaFayette's 1825 tour here, Parker met him at a Utica reception.

THE QUARRY

Sidney Putnam opened the first quarry in 1832 on the site of the Nassimos Co-Op gas station in 2011. The stone was used to build the Congregational Stone Church in 1834, local locks on the Chenango Canal, cellars and lime kilns. The railroad arrived in 1870 to transport the stone replacing the canal and the horse and wagons. The quarry produced the first crushed stone for construction projects in 1872. After Putnam died in 1882, a firm called Putnam and Juhl operated the quarry, and in 1899, F.E. Conley Stone Company was listed as operator. It was considered one of the largest quarries in the state. H.V. Owens and others purchased the stone quarry, then known as Peerless Quarries in 1922, and a new plant was opened just north on Route 12-B, where it still operates today. Tragedy struck the quarry in 1934 when a dynamite explosion killed four employees of Eastern Rock Company. Operators since then have been Eastern Rock, Koppers, Benchmark and Hanson in 2011, which are still taking out stone for road construction and making macadam or colprovia for roads and driveways, etc.

ORISKANY FALLS

Oriskany Falls was first called Cassety Hollow after Colonel Thomas Cassety in 1794. Cassety built a sawmill using the energy from Oriskany Creek. Cassety was a merchant and died in August 1831, at age eighty-four, a melancholy death, according to Pomroy Jones. A clothier had left a bottle of sulfuric acid at Cassety's store. The colonel thought it was whiskey, and the "fatal draught closed his life in a few hours."

Oriskany Falls, incorporated in March 1888, was a busy village during the canal era, with textile mills, flour and gristmills, foundries, machine shops, blacksmith shops, wagon and cooper shops, two sawmills, a stone quarry, Risley & Smith distillery, a brewery that made seven thousand barrels of ale and lager per year, a post office (1829), livery stables, cabinet and furniture makers, undertakers, cigar manufacturers, shoemakers, hotels, coal dealers, newspaper publisher, doctors, dentists, teachers, carpenters and druggists. By 1878, railroads were preferred, and the canal was closed. Towpaths were turned into roads, and sections of the canal were dismantled or abandoned completely.

The 1907 *New Century Atlas* reveals the tempo of the community, with a public school, a railroad station, a coal yard, a sawmill, a gristmill, an opera house, Madison House and Sargent House hotels, four churches (Methodist,

Oriskany Creek just north of Covidien Plant, 2010. State Route 12-B is at right. *Courtesy of Marc R. Goldberg.*

Episcopal, Roman Catholic and Congregational), Hazard Cooperage and various properties of Hatheway & Reynolds Knit Goods, which all made up the Oriskany Falls economy and society.

The C.W. Clark Memorial Library has a rich history that traces back to 1937 when former Oriskany Falls postmaster C.W. Clark died and left his house at 234 North Main Street for the specific purpose to house a library. The library opened a year later with Helen King as librarian; she was succeeded by Stephanie Falbo in 1945 until 1989. Millie Miner, a school librarian, served next, and funding started to come from tax money through the Waterville Central School. In 1961, the library joined the Mid-York Library System. A new era began in 1997 when George Tucker, village philanthropist and generous businessman, gave the former Perry hardware store to the library. After extensive renovations, it opened on October 19, 1997 at 160 North Main Street and continues its service to the village today.

Douglas Memorial Park, between Main and South Main Streets, was originally a basin for the Chenango Canal, whose route was along South Main Street. James A. Douglas was a prominent educator, politician and

Oriskany Falls in the Village of Oriskany Falls, under State Route 12-B bridge. *Courtesy of Marc R. Goldberg.*

businessman until his 1926 death. He owned a warehouse and a brewery and served as village president and town supervisor. He gave land for the park.

From 1897 to 2011, the large brick building between South Main and Madison Streets on Division Street has housed various kinds of manufacturing. Utica Knitting Company, which erected the mill, used creek water for power and used the railroad tracks right next door to ship goods. Utica Knitting built a number of "mill houses" on Madison Street and three on South Main Street around 1913 to give workers a place to live. Many French Canadians from the Tupper Lake, New York area came to work and live in Oriskany Falls. These homes still line Madison Street.

Due to poor economic conditions, the mill shut down in November 1920 but reopened within a year. The depression of the 1930s also caused shutdowns, but it staggered through and made long-legged underwear and children's clothing; it ended operations in 1950. This and many other local cotton mills joined a trend of moving south in the 1950s. In December 1951, a subsidiary of Lily White Sales Company of New York City bought the mill to make sterile bandages, cheesecloth and other products. It was also called Cascade Finishing in the 1950s.

Valley Road, Oriskany Creek, and NYO&W railroad bridge, circa 1940, between Solsville and Oriskany Falls. *Courtesy of Limestone Ridge Historical Society.*

The South Main Street façade of Covidien Plant, Oriskany Falls, 2010. *Courtesy of Marc R. Goldberg.*

Sold again in 1966 to Chesebrough-Ponds, the mill continued with the previous product line, added a large warehouse at the back of the building and employed about 200 workers. Sherwood Medical Company of American Home Products took over in 1986 with some new products. This was a time of high employment at the mill. Changing ownership continued as American Home merged two divisions into Sherwood-Davis & Geck, one of the world's major makers of medical and surgical devices such as needles, syringes, tubes, catheters, wound management products, thermometry and respiratory devices. About 260 were employed by Sherwood- Davis & Geck. Other operators were Tyco and Kendall. Another change happened in 2000 when the name became Covidien Company, but the final blow came in the summer of 2009 when it announced that the plant would close in 2011, thus ending over 110 years of a major manufacturer in Oriskany Falls.

Also in the early 1900s, Hatheway & Reynolds made men's sweaters in a factory on Mill Street, where a fire occurred in 1951. Shaw's Store ran for a few years, but it is now the site of the village public works department and the wastewater treatment plant.

Augusta farmers carried on during the 1800s and early 1900s much like those in neighboring towns, raising wheat, corn and potatoes and keeping ten to twelve dairy cows. Many farms also had hop yards, from which the farmers expected to get some extra cash for the hops. Hops phased out in the early 1900s when a mold developed; dairy and field crops such as corn, soybeans, green beans, and wheat are now grown. About ten dairy farms still operate in 2011 in the town of Augusta. Agriculture has changed dramatically from 150 years ago. Now fewer, but larger, farms use fewer workers, and yields have gone up. Farmers suffer economically from uncontrollable markets— too big for any one farmer to influence.

Education came to Oriskany Falls when one-room common schools taught the 3 R's to neighborhood children within walking distance. A high school at College and Cottage Streets was built in 1891, but it burned in January 1892 and was rebuilt. It was replaced with a more modern school containing kindergarten through grade twelve in 1939. Oriskany Falls had declining enrollment and increasing taxes, which became an incentive to merge with Waterville Central School in 1983. The Oriskany Falls High School graduating class never was too large. Nine graduated in 1927, thirteen in 1943, thirteen in 1947, nine in 1969 and nineteen in 1983, the last graduation prior to merging with Waterville Central. The school had two literary societies in the 1930s: the Athenians and the Ciceronians. They held debates and sponsored entertainment for students and the village residents. While a small school,

Dike and mill in Oriskany Falls, circa 1910. *Courtesy of Mel and Evelyn Edwards.*

both German and French were taught at one time. With no gymnasium large enough, school basketball games took place on the third floor of the McLaughlin Block. Eventually a gym was added to the school. In the 1930s and 1940s, an active alumni association held annual banquets.

The Village of Oriskany Falls in 2011 has a Rotary service club, the United Methodist and St. Joseph's Churches, the Limestone Ridge Historical Society, Alliance Masonic Lodge, Eastern Star, Senior Citizens, Oriskany Falls Fire Department, a bowling alley, gas station, post office, Falls Village Market, Barker Brook nine-hole golf course, three beauty shops, barber shop, laundromat, the American Legion, a family medical practice, a bank, an insurance office, Tallman's Diner, a pizza parlor, some apartment complexes including Oliver Senior Apartments and the Clark Library, plus the standard sports and scouting activities for youth.

At an elevation of 960 feet, the village is situated between several kames on the south and two hills on the north, making the village a narrow passage for the creek that falls 20 feet just east of State Route 12-B.

Floods and fires have caused devastation in Oriskany Falls through the years. Heavy rains on June 11, 1917, broke the Solsville dams, causing a huge stream to rush down the creek and cause major property damage and two deaths in Oriskany Falls. The flood especially hit the village hard, according to an account in the February 1, 1918 *Science*, which was written by a Pennsylvania State University geologist, H. N. Eaton, who was staying in a neighboring town at the time.

Eaton writes:

> *From Solsville to Oriskany Falls, nearly four miles, the stream is constricted within a valley only a few hundred yards wide, choked with kames which expand to the east and north into one of the larger kame areas of central New York. Due to severe and continual rain on the night of June 10, the three ponds (one at Solsville and two east of Solsville near Lyons Mills) broke their dams almost simultaneously about 4 o'clock in the morning. A wave of huge proportions rolled down the narrow valley destroying buildings and ruining crops in its path.*
>
> *Oriskany Falls is situated in the valley between a steep rock hill on the north and a large kame on the south. Fortunately, the inhabitants were warned by telephone, however, two persons were drowned. The flood followed the creek to the southeast and washed away the railroad embankment near the falls. The track was suspended in mid air for at least 100 feet to the bridge.*

This flood prompted an inquest by the Oneida County coroner Dr. W.J. Smith, who held hearings in Solsville. George R. Smith, owner of the Solsville dam, Frank W. Fiske, owner of the next dam to the east, and George A. Lyons, owner of the Lyon's Mills dam, were all called and agreed to the severity of the waters; they all testified that they had "done all in their power to lighten the pressure of water and had given all the warning in their power to the Village of Oriskany Falls." Two men, Albert Talarcizyk and John Conklin, drowned while trying to get a handcar out of rising waters. They both worked for the New York Ontario & Western Railroad. Albert Talarcizyk was the first burial in St. Joseph's Cemetery.

Fires unfortunately make up a large part of Oriskany Falls' history. They occurred in the downtown section over a long period of time. As mentioned earlier, the public school burned in 1892, and the year 1896 saw fires to these structures: two woolen mills, a storehouse, three blocks, the Fowler Block and the corner of North Main and Madison Streets. A power house burned in 1895. In 1909, the Sargent House at College and North Main Streets burned, and in 1952 and 1969, fire devastated the south side of Main Street. In 1952, the Star Theater in the Slotnick Block burned, and in 1958, the bowling alley on Madison Street burned. The Hatheway & Reynolds mill on Mill Street also burned in 1951, ending its run as Shaw's General Store. Two fires in 1969 destroyed the Victory Market, a pharmacy, a laundromat and

Baker & Cole Jewelers. On Halloween night in 1996, the feed mill adjacent to the falls and State Route 12-B (Madison Street) burned.

While a fire department called the Oriskany Falls Firemen's Organization got a charter in 1873, no municipal water system and a lack of hose hindered fighting fires. Since then, the Oriskany Falls Fire Department has grown and moved a few times. Previously, it was located in the current village and town hall at 186 North Main Street but needed more room for larger apparatus. It bought seventeen acres of land in 1968 at 172 Madison Street. A pavilion was put up in 1969, and the new four-bay firehouse was dedicated in 1974. The field days began in 1973 and lasted for thirty years, but they now have been discontinued. Motocross events occurred more recently at the firemen's field, but they are not held anymore

The Bowings and Company of Seneca Falls, New York hand engine was acquired in 1871 and went to the Firemen's Museum in Hudson, New York, after it retired from service. Now it has been returned and completely refurbished by the volunteers. Important to the community—some eighteen miles from Utica hospitals and about ten miles from the smaller Hamilton Hospital—is the fire department ambulance that answers many medical calls and accidents each year.

The landmark 1835 Stone Congregational Church ended its services in May 1958. Other congregations tried unsuccessfully to use it, and now the village owns the church made of local limestone. The village took ownership in 1974, and it was listed on the National Register of Historic Places in 1979.

Oriskany Falls NYO&W Railroad station and engine, circa 1920. *Courtesy of Mel and Evelyn Edwards.*

77

H&R mill, Oriskany Falls, circa 1920. *Courtesy of Mel and Evelyn Edwards.*

The Episcopal Church of the Good Shepherd organized in 1873 and ended services February 10, 1993. The Methodists also came to Oriskany Falls in 1858, held some services at the Stone Congregational Church and bought a building in 1867. They now hold services in their white church with the clock tower at College and North Main Streets, built in 1892. The clock started to keep time for villagers in 1913. St. Joseph's Roman Catholic Church's first sanctuary was on Broad Street. The Catholics built a new church on Main Street in 1923, and today, the rectory and parish center is next door.

Oriskany Falls had a newspaper, the *News*, which began in 1869 with W.E. Phillips as editor and publisher. There was also the *Monthly Advertiser* in 1872 and the *Weekly News*, and both started in the last part of the nineteenth century. The *Oriskany Falls News* lasted until the early 1930s. For much of the twentieth century, the *Waterville Times* collected news of events in Oriskany Falls and continues to do so along with the *Midyork Weekly* from Hamilton.

Businessman George Tucker revived the depressed and fire-worn downtown area in 1970 when he opened a grocery store, Tucker's Big M, and other businesses. He sold the store to the Turner family, who sold to David and Judy Keshler in 2004. In 2006, brothers-in-law Badal Singh and Sukhminder Singh, natives of India, took over the grocery store and gasoline island, which they still operate in 2011.

Preserving local history has been the charge of the Limestone Ridge Historical Society since its founding in 1975. It now occupies the former Church of the Good Shepherd with displays, artifact storage and a research library.

Chapter 8

The Middle Communities

FORGE HOLLOW IN THE TOWN OF MARSHALL

Big Creek squeezes through Forge Hollow in a very narrow channel with cliffs and caves on the west side at an elevation of 980 feet. Forge Hollow is on the former Brothertown Patent and today's State Route 315 between Deansboro and Waterville. A forge and foundry had these operators since 1801: Daniel Hanchett, John Winslow, Thomas Winslow, Ward Winslow and Billy Titus. In 1837, an iron grinding mill of Backus A. Beardsley began, and it was incorporated in 1918 by T. Harold Townsend. In the 1860s, thirty-five houses, a forge, the Universalist church and a dance hall were in Forge Hollow.

Between Forge Hollow and Waterville, there were a gristmill and a sawmill, and at an earlier time, three sawmills and three gristmills used the big drop in the creek to power their operations. On the 1874 atlas map, there was a Universalist church, a hotel and store run by D. Page, a sawmill, a gristmill, furniture shop, a common school, a forge, a blacksmith shop, a triphammer shop, and tannery. In 1874, H.M. Rouse grew teasel and ran a mill to card wool. Fuller's Teasel was formerly widely used in textile processing, providing a natural comb for cleaning, aligning and raising the nap on fabrics, particularly wool. It differs from the wild type in having stouter, somewhat recurved spines on the seed heads. The dried flower heads were attached to spindles, wheels or cylinders, sometimes called teasel frames, to raise the nap on fabrics (that is, to tease the fibers).

Forge Hollow was a thriving village to the mid-1800s, but in 2011 it's a winding section of State Route 315 with about fifteen homes near the creek and a cliff which contains some fossils.

Hops grew around Forge Hollow, as they did throughout the area. A hop extract firm, New York Hop Extract Company, ran between 1875 and 1935 about two miles south of Forge Hollow on the west side of the State Road.

Forge Hollow resident Jim Bogan has romanticized the past along Big Creek with poetry and essays in a 2003 book entitled *Big Creek Valley*. Bogan writes with much nostalgic sentiment about stories of people and places in the valley that he heard about when a child. For example, Brothertown Indian Tom Kindness and his adventures and talents pop up in several stories. Author Jim Bogan's *Big Creek Valley* describes the valley this way: "The valley floor was always deep in shadow long after our hilltop and the barn sides were vivid with sunrise. As summer lengthened there would be a roll of fog that hovered along the creek."

TOWN OF MARSHALL AND HAMLET OF DEANSBORO

Moving downstream from Oriskany Falls, the next Town is Marshall and the hamlet of Deansboro on the former Brothertown Patent. Brothertown Indians settled here in the mid-1780s. A small sliver in the northeast section of Marshall lies on the Seventh Division of the former Coxe Patent.

Originally in the Town of Whitestown and then the Town of Paris, today's Marshall became part of the new Town of Kirkland to the north in 1827. The area finally became its own town on February 21, 1829, and has 19,322 acres, or 32 square miles, within its borders. Townspeople named their community after U.S. Supreme Court chief justice John Marshall, who served between 1801 and 1835. Isaac Miller was the first supervisor, and Levi Buckingham the first town clerk. Joseph Eastman in 1784 and David Barton in 1792 are credited with being the first white settlers.

Most of the Brothertowns were farmers and mill operatives. They became skillful agriculturists, according to Pomroy Jones's 1851 *Annals and Recollections of Oneida County*, and had large and productive fields; quite a proportion of them managed to live very comfortably.

Jones wrote, "But the 'pale-faces' were on their trail, and soon had surrounded their settlement with one hand presenting them with the Bible—the Word of Life—and, with the other, that 'fire-water' their greatest, direst curse, and which was well-known to be death, physical and moral, to the savage."

Deansboro NYO&W Railroad station, 2000. *Courtesy of Marshall Historical Society.*

The Dean family was quite prominent. John S. Dean (1732–1820) in 1795 was sent by the Society of Friends in New York City as a missionary. Dean was to "teach industry and morality." The Town of Brothertown became known as Deansville, appropriately named after Dean and his son, Thomas (1779–1844), who followed him to care for the Indians. Thomas Dean owned the Friends Cotton and Woolen Manufactory and served as Indian agent, too. Both Deans are buried side by side in the Deansboro Cemetery. Thomas became an attorney, teacher, postmaster, owner of several farms and a trustee of Hamilton College, from which his oldest son, John, graduated in 1832.

A wing of the Dean homestead was built about 1799 as the Indian agent's office, but the main section was built by Brothertowns for Dean in 1824. The Dean Homestead is situated at West Hill Road and State Route 12-B on lot 15 of the Brothertown Patent. It was owned by Indian Elijah Wampy Jr., but with permission from the state legislature, Dean bought it in 1827 with twenty-nine acres. The current owner is Parke Investment Company, which also owns the Deansboro Hotel next door.

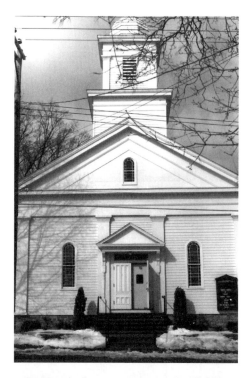

Deansboro churches: United Methodist Church is at bottom and United Church of Christ is at top. *Courtesy of Marshall Historical Society.*

Thomas Dean traveled west to arrange for a new home for the Brothertowns. The Brothertowns were vulnerable to diseases, land encroachment and disastrous temptations of alcohol, which caused most of them to move west to Wisconsin after 1830. They landed on a reservation in Calumet County on the east side of Lake Winnebago in Wisconsin. In 1839, the Indians were granted citizenship and lost their land and tribal status. Most were gone from Marshall by 1848, but in 1907, Romance Wyatt—the last Brothertown—died and was buried in the Deansboro Cemetery.

Besides the Dean Homestead, another interesting house, dating from the 1850s, just north of Deansboro on the west side of State Route 12-B is the octagon house, one of the few eight-sided homes in the area. It is of wood construction and has a large porch across the front. Orson Fowler (1809–1887) of Cohocton, New York, published an architectural book about octagon houses, where he maintained that the octagon style was cheaper, roomier and more convenient since there were no dark corners. Fowler's book was *A Home for All.*

The Utica, Clinton and Binghamton Railroad (later the New York Ontario & Western Railroad) reached Deansville in 1867 and put up a railroad station with vertical siding and large overhangs, typical of the railroad architecture of the late 1860s. It was used from 1867 to 1957 when the NYO&W ended. Listed on National Register of Historic Places in 2002, it is owned by three Deansboro men and may be a museum some day.

Religion in Deansboro has remained constant for over two hundred years. The United Methodist church began as classes back in 1803, but the church was not built until 1837. It burned in 1883, and the present church was built a year later; it remains a part of Deansboro cultural scene. The church contains an eight-day, three-face town clock in its tower. North on State Route 12-B is the United Church of Christ. It was originally the Deansboro Congregational Church, which traces itself back to 1797 at Hanover, but this church was not built until 1853. Both churches hold regular services and also old-fashioned church suppers, bazaars and rummage sales. Earlier, in the nineteenth century in the Town of Marshall, both Hanover and Forge Hollow had churches.

In the mid-1800s, the hamlet of Deansville had one gristmill, two lime kilns, one blacksmith shop and the Deansville Hotel, run by A. Van Valkenburg. Van Slyke & May Company made carriages, sleighs and wagons on the Chenango Canal near Kirkland/Marshall town line. The 1850 U.S. census for the entire Town of Marshall listed 10 common school districts, with 1,400 volumes of books, 1 distillery, 4 blacksmith shops, 1 boot maker,

Deansboro Milk Plant, State Route 315, circa 1935. *Courtesy of Marshall Historical Society.*

4 iron forgers, 1 wagon maker, 2 gristmills, 4 sawmills, 1 churn maker and 1 woolen mill.

Deansboro in the 1910s had a grist- and cider mill, an electric plant, U.S. Condensed Milk Company, Deansboro Creamery, a cooper shop, the NYO&W Railroad and station, the Barton Hose Company firehouse, Deansboro Association Hall (earlier the Maccabee Hall), a school on the West Hill Road, the hotel and the two churches. To provide for the farmers, the Moses Cronk feed mill (1897 to a 1960s fire) and Hinman feed mill operated into the 1950s, when it burned. Both were off State Route 315—the road to Waterville.

The Deansboro Condensery, or milk station at the tracks, was opened by George I. Hovey in 1902 or 1903 and closed in April 1983 as the farm sector declined. It outlasted the milk plants in Oriskany Falls, Clinton, Marshall Station and Waterville. Some 180 patrons supplied raw milk and used ten-gallon cans until 1977, when bulk tanks were required. By the 1930s, the plant had twenty-five employees and owned three or four tenant houses. A 125-foot chimney dominated the Deansboro skyscape. Claude and Grove Hinman acquired the plant in 1933 and renamed it Hinman Farm Products, manufacturing dry milk along with liquid milk. New York City was the main market via railroad until the plant closed in 1957, and then tank trucks transported the milk.

Other businesses to sell to famers were J.C. Earl and Northrup, which sold farm machinery. Previously, hops were big until the 1920s, and now

Barton Hose Company, Deansboro, circa 1910. It was located on the east side of State Route 12-B. *Courtesy of Marshall Historical Society.*

dairy farms predominate, along with some potatoes, sweet corn, pumpkins, cabbage and squash.

The Barton Hose Company began in 1906. The current firehouse was built in 1957, and a second story was added in 2000 for the Deansboro Fire Department.

A ridge of limestone has allowed quarrying since the early days at the current Hanson site just north of Oriskany Falls but in the Town of Marshall. A quarry was operated by Cittadino at Paris Hill in the twentieth century. Dawes, Zwiefel and Schachtlers also had small quarries off Shanley Road.

Although the Deansboro elevation is 795 feet above sea level, the Town of Marshall boasts the highest point in Oneida County on Tassel Hill, in the southeast section of the town, at 2,100 feet. Turkey Creek, a tributary of the Oriskany, has the picturesque—though seldom seen—Turkey Falls south of Shanley Road in the Town of Marshall. Turkey Creek joins Oriskany Creek at the second bridge in the Dugway.

The name of the hamlet changed from Deansville to Deansboro in 1894 due to post office confusion with Dansville, New York, south of Rochester. The Deansboro Centennial took place in 1994 with an appropriate book and parade.

Deansboro had three plank roads: 1) Utica, via Clinton and Deansville, to Waterville (1849–1872); 2) Waterville to Utica through Hanover and Paris Hill; and 3) Deansboro to Hamilton (1848–1874). By the 1870s, the plank road era of private stock companies and toll houses had ended. Bus service arrived in Deansboro as early as 1913 with the Clinton/Deansboro/Waterville bus line. This began in Clinton where the Utica trolley line ended.

In the mid-twentieth century, Deansboro boasted a Home Bureau organization and a Garden Club, activities for women. The Garden Club held a vegetable and flower fair at the school and sold plants and seeds annually. The home bureau had meetings on topics such as sewing, braided rugs, mending and darning and metal trays.

Deansboro Post Office, on the east side of State Route 12-B, circa 1915. *Courtesy of Marshall Historical Society.*

Maccabee Hall on State Route 315 was originally owned by the Knights of the Maccabees when built in 1897. The Maccabees left the hall in the 1920s, and others later owned it. In 1931, when the public school burned, classes were held there. For a while in the 1970s, a bar ran in the lower level. The Barton Hose Company owned it for a time, too. It burned in 1981 and has been razed.

The Maccabees were a fraternal order with local chapters called "Tents" and was founded in 1878 in London, Ontario, as a mutual assessment society. Each member pledged to donate ten cents to the widow of a deceased "brother." Edgar Lamont Bumpus graduated from Hamilton College in 1881 and, after a brief teaching stint, became an area organizer and recruiter for the Maccabees. Tents were also located in Clinton, Utica, Westmoreland, Deansboro and West Winfield.

The hamlet of Deansboro contains, in 2011, the Marshall town offices at 2651 State Route 12-B in the former Deansboro public school, which

Deansboro Civilian Conservation Corps camp. State Route 12-B was about one mile south, circa 1940. *Courtesy of Marshall Historical Society.*

merged with Waterville in 1931. Prior to a 1931 fire, the public school was on West Hill. Classes were held in the Deansboro school after the merger with Waterville Central until the 1950s. Then the Town of Marshall purchased it for town offices; they are still used today.

Small shops, garages, a diner, a tavern, a corner superette, a motorcycle garage, Marshall Historical Society, the Deansboro Hotel, a library and several dairy farms constitute Deansboro's economy in 2011. With its recently upgraded water system, a lighting and fire district, Deansboro has some of the amenities of larger suburbs while maintaining a distinct rural small-town ambience.

Mostly rural Marshall is laced with many fine-appearing farms today in the Hanover area and southern parts of the town. In 1880, 280 farms raised hops. Now around thirty farmers still maintain dairies and raise field crops, too. Two farmers, the Barkers and McConnells, trace their farms back to founding ancestors Wardwell Barker in 1795 and Thaddeus McConnell in 1796. The families still run farms and dairies some 215 years later.

The Musical Museum between 1948 and 1998 was a unique tourist attraction in Deansboro. Its several rooms housed the Sanders family collection of restored musical instruments such as organs, pianos, nickelodeons, etc. Some of these dated back to the 1500s, and tourists could put in their nickels and quarters to hear the music.

Clinton/Deansboro/Waterville bus at Clinton Park, circa 1923. *Courtesy of Clinton Historical Society.*

Since 1896, Deansboro has had a privately owned water system from a small reservoir and now a water tank on the West Hills. A water district has been established, with mains carrying the water to 140 customers. The water was chlorinated starting in 1946, and in 1997, a sand infiltration system was installed.

Deansboro had something unique for the Oriskany Valley—a Civilian Conservation Corps (CCC) camp just south of the hamlet near Hughes Road on the west side of State Route 12-B at the curve. The CCC, one of the New Deal's alphabet agencies to create jobs, had a camp there from the late 1930s until the early 1940s. The young men engaged in conservation projects around the area. During World War II, when labor to pick crops was scarce, several Jamaican men were brought in and lived at the camp in pretty crude conditions.

Many three- to four-corner hamlets, which have seen more active days, show up on old maps in the Town of Marshall: Dicksville, Forge Hollow, Brothertown, Moore's Corners, Peck's Corners, McConnell's Corners, Hubbard's Corners, Hanover Green and Daytonville.

Town of Kirkland

In the Town of Kirkland, Oriskany Creek flows through Farmer's Mills (Milburn), Franklin Springs, Clinton, Kirkland and Clark Mills. Today's Town of Kirkland was on part of the Sixth Division of Coxe Patent, on parts of the Brothertown Patent, and on Oneida Indian land prior to the Revolutionary War.

White men, led by Revolutionary War captain Moses Foote from Plymouth, Connecticut, came to Kirkland in March 1787 when seven families settled here. This was in the Town of German Flatts at that time and in Montgomery County. Feeling their isolation and their lack of organization, they drew up a sort of compact for the regulation of affairs, which they all signed and agreed to abide to the terms.

Centering on the Village of Clinton, more settlers came, and farming occupied many of them, along with local tradesmen such as blacksmiths, millers, joiners, potters and sawyers, etc. Kirkland developed as an agricultural region featuring numerous small farms with Clinton as the hub and mercantile center.

The Town of Kirkland was formed from the Town of Paris on April 13, 1827, and today has a four-person town board, a supervisor, a town clerk and a highway superintendent. Also elected are the tax collector and two

Town of Kirkland Municipal Building and Highway Garage, located on State Route 12-B, Franklin Springs, 2010. *Courtesy of Marc R. Goldberg.*

justices of the peace. Several appointed officials and employees serve the residents, too: police officers, assessor, planning officer, sanitary and building inspector, parks, highway and rink employees.

Beginning mainly as a self-sufficient farming community, Kirkland was known for fruit cultivation in the mid-1800s. In the early twentieth century, hop yards were numerous, especially on the road to Deansboro. Kirkland also had a woolen mill, creameries, cheese factories, milk stations, cotton mills, cider mills, a furniture polish maker and the Lithia water industry; it also boasted the founding of Bristol-Myers-Squibb Company in 1887.

Clinton hematite iron ore was discovered by a farmhand in 1797, and mining became a large industry. Two blast furnaces were built and operated on and off between 1851 and 1913, one in Kirkland on State Route 5 at Oriskany Creek and one in Franklin Iron Works off Furnace Street. Mining declined here when the Mesabi Range opened, and Clinton's lower grade ore fell out of favor with the steel industry. However, mining did continue on a smaller scale until 1963, when the last mine, owned by Pfizer Company, on Brimfield Street closed. Between 1913 and 1963, the hematite ore went directly to the Clinton Metallic Paint Company in Franklin Springs for use as pigmentation in paints and mortar colors.

In the twentieth century, the Kirkland farm and manufacturing sectors declined, so that, in 2011, only Rofin Company in Clark Mills, James Rhodes

Company in Franklin Springs, Riverhawk Company on Utica Road and Indium Company on Robinson Road in Clinton represent the remaining Kirkland manufacturing sector.

Only about eighteen to twenty farms operate within the town in 2011, and they are mostly dairy farms that also raise corn, hay, oats, wheat and soybeans. Kirkland is not the bustling farming hub of one hundred years ago, when feed mills, gristmills, milk stations, cheese factories, hop cultivation and a Clinton Grange chapter occupied hundreds of residents.

From crude foot trails to ox wagon trails, transportation gradually improved, allowing products and people to move around. The Seneca Turnpike went through on today's State Route 5 around 1795, and a plank road reached Clinton on the way to Deansboro and Waterville in 1849. The coming of the Chenango Canal in 1836 and the railroad in 1867 made Kirkland open to bigger markets. The Utica, Clinton and Binghamton Railroad, later the New York Ontario & Western Railroad, ended in bankruptcy in 1957. Passenger service had stopped in the 1920s. The spring to fall nature of the Chenango Canal allowed bulk goods such as iron ore, limestone and coal to go from source to market part of the year.

The three main employers currently in the town are the Clinton Central Schools, Lutheran Cares Ministries and Hamilton College, with many others working in stores, banks, garages, farms and for the town and village governments. Many Kirkland residents commute to Utica, Syracuse and Rome daily for work. A newer feature of Kirkland is the number of retirement-age residents and special facilities for them, such as Clinton Manor, the Villas and garden apartments.

Ice hockey arrived in Kirkland in 1917 when Albert I. Prettyman began his coaching career at Hamilton College. Village boys quickly took up the sport. A high school team and an adult hockey team began in the late 1920s, and an outdoor rink was created on Meadow Street. The Clinton Comets competed in the semipro Eastern Hockey League in the 1950s and 1960s. Portions of the movie *Slapshot* with Paul Newman were filmed here in the mid-1970s.

The first Clinton Arena was built in 1948 for indoor hockey and figure skating. In 2011, two ice rinks were within the Town of Kirkland, Sage Rink at Hamilton and the Clinton Arena, now owned by the Town of Kirkland, on Kirkland Avenue. Few other towns of ten thousand people can claim this.

The land of Kirkland has the rich Oriskany bottom soil for farming, but hills ascend on each side of the valley. Prospect Point off Skyline Drive on the west is at a height of 1,378 feet above sea level. Red Hill, east of Chuckery, is 1,250 feet above sea level. The Town of Kirkland has about

Clinton Arena, built 1953–1954, Kirkland Avenue, 2010. *Courtesy of Marc R. Goldberg.*

ten thousand inhabitants, according to the 2000 census, with two thousand living within the Village of Clinton. The town collects about $6 million a year from various taxes and fees.

FARMER'S MILLS (MILBURN)

In the Town of Kirkland on the corner of Sawyer Road and Dugway Road is Farmer's Mills, called Milburn in the early 1900s. This area is also called the Dugway, because of the sharp cliff beside the Oriskany as it flows through a narrow channel. Red shale lines the sides of the cliff, which rises about ninety feet above the creek to a farmer's flat field.

The creek runs east and then curves sharply north there. It was the site of two sawmills, a gristmill, a cotton batting mill, a triphammer shop, a blacksmith shop, etc., in the 1800s. The creek's water power turned the wheels in these shops and mills. Turkey Creek empties into the Oriskany just south of the second bridge.

Red Bridge in Dugway, circa 1915. *Courtesy of Clinton Historical Society.*

In 1861, Willard H. Healy advertised in the *Clinton Courier* for custom grinding and flouring done on "short notice"—"hard cash" was paid for all kinds of grain at the highest market value; deliveries were free of charge. Buckwheat was ground every day except Sunday, and corn on the ear and oats were always on hand, according to the advertisement.

The above businesses faded away by the 1900s, as the times and technology changed. Farmer's Mills had a migrant camp in the 1950s that housed southern blacks who came in the summer to pick the beans and peas. This camp caused many complaints of noise, fights and unsanitary conditions from neighboring residents. In 2011, Farmer's Mills has the creek, two bridges and less than ten homes. Trout fishermen visit each spring and summer, but the small hamlet is a far cry from the busy hive of commerce of the 1800s.

FRANKLIN SPRINGS

Situated about one mile south of Clinton in the Oriskany Valley is the hamlet of Franklin Springs—"Franklin" on an 1830 map and "Franklin Iron Works" on maps between 1850 and 1895. This specific area was part of the Brothertown Indian land at first.

At an elevation of 620 feet, Franklin Springs has had a varied business history with a blast furnace and a lithia water bottling industry. About

James Rhodes plant, located on State Route 12-B in Franklin Springs, 2010. *Courtesy of Marc R. Goldberg.*

two years after Clinton began in 1787, Levi Barker and his family started the settlement. Levi's son, Lester, was the first white person born west of the 1768 Fort Stanwix Treaty Line. A daughter, Louisa M. Barker, went on to teach at the Clinton Liberal Institute between 1840 and 1851. She founded two girls' schools in Clinton: Home Cottage Seminary in 1854 and Cottage Seminary.

Gordon's *Gazetteer* of 1836 described Franklin as having one sawmill, one tavern, two stores and fifteen dwellings. Things changed in 1851 when the blast furnace was erected. By 1860, thirty-five houses were occupied, and twenty-four of them were blast furnace "company" homes. Three saloons, two schools, two boarding hotels, a company store, a railroad station and an icehouse composed the economic base during the heyday of the blast furnace. No church ever existed in the hamlet. Bible students will be amused, or alarmed, to discover that this hamlet was also referred to as "Sodom" as late as the 1870s in the *Clinton Courier*.

Clinton hematite iron ore was brought by wagon, canalboat and, after 1867, by railroad from the east side of Clinton to the furnace. Coal arrived

Creek in Dugway, a view east at second bridge over Lumbard Road, 2010. *Courtesy of Marc R. Goldberg.*

from Pennsylvania, while limestone came from local quarries to make the cast-iron. Miners and furnace workers were an ethnic mix of Poles, Welsh and Hungarians, plus local men and off-season farmhands. Furnace Street had many homes built for the workers that now are mostly gone. Slag piles from the iron process and the old mill pond depression may still be seen as remnants of the once-prosperous community.

Franklin also had a sawmill, a post office, a train station, a hotel, a store and a school across from the American Legion in the mid-1800s. A cheese factory on the east side of the road produced 100,630 pounds of cheese in 1866 at a market value of $17,310.89. The Clinton Metallic Paint Company began in 1886 on White Creek, producing red barn paint and mortar colors. It closed in 1964, and in 2011, James Rhodes Company makes electrical components in an expanded complex. The lithia water business took over for the declining blast furnace operations after Fred Suppe discovered the water on his Dugway Road hop farm in 1888. Seven firms bottled the water for drinking and into soft drinks such as birch beer and ginger beer. The last one, Split-Rock Company, closed in the early 1970s and had been operated by a Kernan family from Utica.

Angler sign in fishing access area at second bridge in Dugway, 2010. *Courtesy of Marc R. Goldberg.*

Indicative of the changing economy, the Franklin Iron Works post office changed to Franklin Springs in 1898.

Franklin Springs today has a smaller economic base than previously. A used-car dealer, the American Legion, a physical therapist, the post office (since 1867), a gun dealer, the Clinton Tractor trailer sales lot, a garage, James Rhodes Company, the town highway garage and town offices make up the hamlet's activities.

The grandeur of the blast furnace lighting up the night sky, when pouring off a batch of molten iron, has been long gone, as are most other enterprises in Franklin Springs. It's a quiet and pleasant southern neighbor to Clinton with twenty-five to thirty homes intersected by State Route 12-B, Post Street and Grant Road.

This incident, found in the January 27, 1881 edition of the *Clinton Courier*, describes a nonroutine day in the life of an innkeeper in the 1880s in Franklin Iron Works:

"Franklin Hotel Burlgary story": The hotel, kept by William H. Clark, was the scene of a lively encounter last Saturday. Awakened by noise in the bedroom Mrs. Clark discovered a man creeping on all fours toward the bed. Aroused, Mr. Clark jumped out of bed and made chase of the villain and overtook him. Mr. Clark managed to give a sample of his fully-developed muscle on the side of the intruder's head knocking him head over heels, then seizing a rocking chair at hand, dealt him repeated blows till the chair was reduced to kindling wood, and the burglar glad to lie still at his command. With a revolver cocked, ready to use if he made a move, Mr. Clark called for Constable J.Q. Adams, who soon arrived and placed handcuffs on him and took him to the lockup. The culprit gave his name as Patrick McLaughlin from Oriskany Falls; he had recently served five years in prison. Found in McLaughlin's pockets were a gold watch, chain, locket, pin, and other valuable jewelry worth over $100.00. It is not likely the hotel at Franklin will be troubled again by such a visitor while Mr. Clark is proprietor.

VILLAGE OF CLINTON

In 1813, the *Spafford Gazetteer of New York* said, "Clinton Village had 55 houses, an Academy (Hamilton College), a meeting house (Old White Meeting House in the Park), some mills, and a post office since 1802."

According to *French's Gazetteer* of 1860, Clinton had five churches—Universalist (1821), Baptist (1832), Methodist (1842), Roman Catholic (1850), Episcopal (1862)—two newspaper offices, a few manufactories, a grammar school, a boarding and high school and a population of 1,174.

The *Clinton Courier* description from 1850 said that,

"There is a good deal of taste displayed by the inhabitants in their Park and Fountain, as well as in building, yards, shrubbery, and shade trees." Further that "all their improvements make it a desirable place for the man of wealth or one of in easy circumstances, to locate and train up his family to future usefulness in its seats of learning and different places of worship."

The *Clinton Courier* of February 15, 1866, described residents of the Town of Paris, from which Kirkland was taken in 1827, as "chiefly of Yankee origin, keen, shrewd, and calculating and for the most part are well-to-do farmers."

West Park Row, Clinton, 2009, a view north from tower of Stone Presbyterian Church. The park is on the right. *Courtesy of Marc R. Goldberg.*

In the 1850 census, Kirkland had 14 common school districts, serving 817 pupils, with a total of 2,039 books, averaging 145 books per common school. Additionally, over 60 private schools, sometimes called "seminaries," operated in Clinton in the nineteenth century prior to the public secondary school movement. Out-of-town and rural students often boarded at the schools or with Clinton families while day students also attended. Some schools lasted for a few years, while others taught students from twenty to seventy years. Notable students here included Leland Stanford, founder of California's Stanford University and railroad tycoon; Clara Barton, Red Cross founder; Grover Cleveland, American president, 1885–1889 and 1893–1895; and Matilda Joslyn Gage, a leading abolitionist and women's right-to-vote advocate.

Elihu Root (February 15, 1845–January 7, 1937), secretary of war and secretary of state under Presidents McKinley and Roosevelt, was born in a building at Hamilton College and is probably Clinton's most famous son. A graduate of Hamilton College and New York University Law School, he received the Nobel Peace Prize in 1912 and was buried in the Hamilton College Cemetery. Controversial poet Ezra Pound and behavioral psychologist B.F.

Clinton Central School, built in 1932. *Courtesy of Mel and Evelyn Edwards.*

Skinner went to Hamilton College, and the college astronomer in the 1880s was Danish-born Christian Heinrich Friedrich Peters, who discovered forty-eight asteroids.

Clinton Mills was on Norton Avenue at Oriskany Creek and was operated by Willard H. Healy in the 1860s. Custom flouring work was done, and Healy had on hand Genesee wheat, graham flour, cracked wheat, oats, cornmeal and buckwheat flour. In 1886, a new knitting mill was in business at the former Clinton Factory mill on Norton Avenue at the creek, formerly owned by Clarks Mills Manufacturing Company. The Clinton Knitting Mill operated between 1904 and 1951, making men's sweaters and bathing suits on Kirkland Avenue, where today's Clinton House apartments are located.

Undertaker L.M. Smith advertised in the February 14, 1861 *Clinton Courier* "metallic burial cases," coffin trimmings and wood coffins, ranging in price from five dollars to thirty-five dollars. He had a new hearse and asked that those sending coffin measurements should "be careful to give the exact measure of the deceased across the breast."

The Reverend Samuel Kirkland was a missionary to the Seneca and Oneida Indians, starting in 1760s and until his death in 1808. He also was an interpreter and diplomat between the Indians and the whites at various land treaties. He helped keep Oneidas and Tuscaroras on the side of colonists during the Revolutionary War. Kirkland became a major land owner when New York state and the Oneidas gave him four thousand acres in 1788.

Kirkland dreamed of teaching Indian youth the white men's ways, so he started the Hamilton-Oneida Academy on College Hill in 1793. He gave three hundred acres of his Kirkland Patent land to the academy, which built a school building and educated several white youth. Few, if any, Indians attended very long. The academy trustees applied to be a college, and the Regents of New York State granted Hamilton College its charter in May 1812. This makes Hamilton the third oldest liberal arts college in the state after Columbia and Union.

Between 1890 and 1920, a few gold cure sanitariums operated in Clinton. These were treatments for alcoholism, drugs and nervousness. Patients would live in the buildings for four weeks and hopefully be cured. This was part of a nationwide trend, as many sanitariums opened across the country. Prohibition basically ended the movement.

The Village of Clinton bustles in 2011 with numerous volunteer-run organizations, a viable downtown business district, a historic district on the National and State Registers of Historic Places; the Clinton Arena; Boynton Pool; Kiwanis, Lions and Rotary service clubs; the Clinton Fire Department; VFW; American Legion; Monday Club; Garden Club; Questers; and youth soccer, baseball, hockey, football and scouting.

The Kirkland Art Center, founded in 1960, occupies the former Clinton Methodist Church on East Park Row, and the Clinton Historical Society, founded in 1962, has its quarters in the former Clinton Baptist Church at 1 Fountain Street. The Academy of Performing & Creative Arts began in 2005 off Taylor Avenue. It holds classes and concerts for children and adults. The Clinton Chamber of Commerce organizes a summer farmers' market, a Thanksgiving Shoppers' Stroll, summer band concerts and other promotions.

Organized religion has changed over the years, as the Clinton United Methodist Church left the village in 1965 for 105 Utica Road. The Stone Presbyterian, St. James Episcopal, and St. Mary's Churches remain in the village. The Resurrection Assembly of God built a new church on Kirkland Avenue in 2004. Currently, a religious group meets Sundays in Lumbard Town Hall. Other congregations have used the second floor of Lumbard since the late 1940s when the Reverend Roger Bates led a group. The Quakers have had a church on Austin Road for over twenty years. The Life in Christ Family Church has a building at 25 Robinson Road. Gone are the Baptists and the Universalists.

Manchester/Kirkland

Two miles north of Clinton is the hamlet of Kirkland, formerly called Manchester in the early to mid-1800s. It's on State Route 5 or the Seneca Turnpike. A post office (1815–1941), cotton mill (1816), a flour mill (1818), a creamery (1852), a cheese factory and the Clinton Iron Ore Company blast furnace from the 1870s to 1913 provided an economic base for the community in the nineteenth century.

The first settler, Robert Parks, built a frame house in 1788, and in 1795, the first burial in the Manchester Cemetery took place. Farming took the time of most settlers, and two taverns plus a store were early operations. Religion arrived in 1834 when the Congregational church (later the Kirkland Presbyterian Church) opened to serve the spiritual needs of the hamlet.

Being right on the Seneca Turnpike helped Manchester (Kirkland) grow with one cotton mill, one gristmill, two taverns, two stores and thirty-five dwellings in 1836. By 1851, Kirkland had two taverns, two stores, a church and a cotton mill, and by the 1870s, two one-room school houses educated the youth.

Kirkland Post Office and General Store of Mrs. Grace Woolnough Wood, located on State Route 5, circa 1920. *Courtesy of Clinton Historical Society.*

Manchester Sheeting Company had 30 employees in 1836 and made 30,000 yards annually. During the 1850–1851 years, it had 4,200 spindles, 100 looms, 120 workers employed and made 11,000,000 yards annually. The mill used 360,000 pounds of cotton prior to burning in 1854. About 35 dairies supplied milk to a cheese factory at the outbreak of the Civil War, making butter and cheese, and by 1874, it used the milk of 450 cows.

An iron ore blast furnace came to Kirkland in 1873 when the Clinton Iron Works opened with $100,000 of common stock. It was on the site of a former cotton mill on the Seneca Turnpike at Oriskany Creek. Theodore W. Dwight was president, and Theodore Avery was secretary and treasurer. A dike was just south of the turnpike, which diverted the water for use in the furnace. A sluiceway could still be seen a few years ago where the water returned to the creek. The wheel house was 36 by 40 feet, the stack house was 60 by 100 feet, the cast house was 50 by 110 feet and the stack itself rose 48 feet above the hearth. This was a substantial complex but never too successful. It had to close at times depending on the economy. It would reopen, but it was declared insolvent in 1890 and closed for good in 1893. It was razed in 1913, the same year as the Franklin Iron Works.

The Rome & Clinton Railroad crossed the Seneca Turnpike in 1872, providing passenger and freight service to Kirkland. The *Gaffney Directory* of 1884 listed Patrick Lynch and A. Youngs, blacksmiths; John Mynch, coal dealer; Albert Kellogg, constable; M.H. Schermerhorn, general store; James Coombs and Thomas Joy, hotels; C.A. Mitchell, meat market; and the iron works.

Flooding for years at Kirkland on the Oriskany has been a headache for local property owners, Kirkland Town Board members and travelers who were detoured around the area until the water receded. The problem is caused by silt buildup on the creek bottom and development on Kirkland Avenue and Route 5, displacing and redirecting the water from the floodplain.

The social activity of Kirkland centered on two dance halls and an athletic field before and during Prohibition in the twentieth century. In 1908, a football game was played there between a Clark Mills squad and Hamilton College, and Clark Mills won and "gained a far-flung reputation as a crack club."

The *Clinton Courier & Chief* of April 1859 reported this story:

> *A correspondent writes of a dastardly attempt of some drunken rowdies to tar and feather Mr. Diefendorf, late keeper of the hotel in Manchester (Kirkland). The contemplated outrage was provoked by the firmness of the landlord in refusing to furnish the rowdies with liquor when in a state of intoxication. They had gone so far as to procure the materials for the*

One-room schoolhouse, built in the 1880s, located on State Route 5, Kirkland. In 2011, it was the Half-Pint Nursery School. *Courtesy of Marc R. Goldberg.*

purpose, and to give the signal for proceedings to commence, when Mr. Diefendorf escaped. We are sorry to report such things in our own town.

After World War II, Kirkland had Harrison's Furniture Store, two fruit stands, three gas stations and a pea vinery. The Kirkland Presbyterian Church closed in 1965. Ten years later, four gas stations, one flea market, five restaurants, two stores, a mobile home lot, an antique store in the former church and a vegetable transfer station and nursery made up Kirkland's commercial base.

The Kirkland commercial area strip on Route 5 has seen better days, with some buildings razed and annual flooding discouraging others from putting money into new businesses there. The Bryne Dairy Store, two used-car dealers, an ice cream/miniature golf course, a barber shop, two restaurants, an investment agency, a small shopping mall, a car detailing shop, a rental storage facility and a landscaping business operate in Kirkland in 2011. Pheasant Run, a townhouse apartment complex, opened in 2006 on Clinton Street just north of Kirkland.

In recent years, plans to bring Utica water to Kirkland have been tied up in legal battles between the Upper Mohawk Valley Water Board and the State Canal Corporation over the availability of Hinckley Reservoir water. Currently Utica water comes along Seneca Turnpike from New Hartford and turns north on Clinton Street to Clark Mills. This leaves most of Kirkland west of Clinton Street without municipal water.

Hopefully Kirkland will revive in appearance and in businesses, and the state Department of Environmental Conservation will allow dredging of Oriskany Creek. Now the DEC's position remains that the creek as a fishery is more important than controlling floods each spring.

CLARK MILLS

Moving north from Kirkland, "Clark's" Mills, as it was called in the mid-1800s, dates from 1789 when Josiah Stillman settled just north of the intersection of Westmoreland and Whitesboro Roads at Stillman Corners on the west side of the road. Other accounts claim that Nathan Thompson settled in the 1790s and built a sawmill and a gristmill in the area off Maple Street. The old Manchester Cemetery burial list has Nathan Thompson, who died in 1826, and his two wives, so we can assume that he moved to Manchester on the Seneca Turnpike and left Clark Mills.

Noah Clark then came here later in 1791 and bought land. Noah had served in the Revolutionary War and saw the surrender of General Charles Cornwallis at Yorktown in 1781. Clark died in Kirkland in July 1851, and his wife, Suze, six years earlier; both are buried in the Kirkland Cemetery on French Road. Noah's son, Ezra Clark, had six children, and in 1846, three of the sons—Ralph, Eneas, and Ammi Bailey—built a cotton mill, 275 feet by 70 feet, on Oriskany Creek and a dike a quarter mile upstream. The dike diverted water to a sluiceway to power the 110 looms. About 250 people worked there by 1874, and 1,750,000 yards of cotton were produced annually. A new dye house, 50 by 144 feet, was built in 1886 at the cotton factory.

French's Gazetteer listed, in Clark's Mills in 1860, forty houses, a post office (since 1858), a gristmill, a sawmill and the Clark's cotton factory complex. Population reached 420 in 1874, including 7 colored people. That year, Clark Mills had a railroad depot, a lumberyard, a store, a batting mill, a school, a harness shop and the Clark Brothers cotton factory.

Ralph and Eneas Clark died a few months apart in early 1873, and Ammi Bailey decided to retire from management and sell out his interest. He

St. Mark's Episcopal
Church, White
Street, Clark Mills,
built in 1863–64.
This photo was taken
in 2010. *Courtesy of
Marc R. Goldberg.*

went to Bloomfield, New Jersey, and worked with his son-in-law to build an
"airline" railway between New York and Philadelphia. Ammi Bailey Clark
died on Valentine's Day in 1883 and was buried with his wife, Mary Brainer,
in Somerset, New Jersey. The mills reorganized with W.A. Hageman of New
York City as president in May 1873 and continued for several years, but
production declined in the 1880s, and the mills closed in 1890.

Immigrants from England had arrived to work in the cotton mill and
formed a chapter of the Order of St. George, played cricket games and
drank tea. St. Mark's Episcopal Church had been built on White Street in
1865 to serve the former Anglicans. More English immigrants moved to
Clark's Mills after 1890, as Yorkshire, England businessman Arthur Hind
formed the Hind Harrison Plush Company and took over the abandoned
factories. More company homes were built for the workers. The plant made
plush for women's coats, casket linings and, later on, car seat upholstery,
employing up to three hundred hands at times.

One footnote about Arthur Hind, a serious stamp collector: he owned
from 1922 to his death in 1933 the famous and rarest stamp in the world,
the 1856 Penny Magenta of British Guiana, which was worth $32,500 then.
It was purchased for $935,000 in 1980 by John DuPont of Philadelphia,
who shot and killed Olympic wrestler David Schultz in 1996. DuPont died
in December 2010 in a Pennsylvania hospital for the criminally insane. It's
assumed the stamp is in a bank vault somewhere.

Hind Harrison Plush ended in 1943 when it was sold to Max Grant, a
Providence, Rhode Island mill agent. The *Utica Daily Press* of August 6,

Hind & Harrison General Store, facing Main Street, circa 1920s, Clark Mills. *Courtesy of Mel and Evelyn Edwards.*

1943, called Grant "a man of substance with many interests in textiles." William R. Kennish was president, but the trend of cotton mills going south crimped the business prospects. The mills finally closed in 1947–1948 and remained vacant for several years.

Major parts of the old mills were razed by Oneida County as a public hazard in 1972, except for Rome Turney Radiator and the old general store. Winns Furniture had expanded and sold household goods until the 1990s. Rich Plan food service currently uses sections of the old store. Since 2008, when Rome Turney Radiator left, its buildings have been taken over by Rofin Company, a maker of heat exchangers similar to Rome Turney. Rofin has plants in both Rome and Clark Mills and provides cooling exchangers for the power plant industry; it is a major supplier to Siemens Company. Rofin has shipped heat exchangers to Europe, as an example of its customers' worldwide range.

Three railroads served Clark Mills between 1900 and 1957: the Rome and Clinton, the West Shore and the Third Rail, an electric interurban service between Utica and Syracuse. Now, the railroads are gone, the mill looms don't exist and the hustle and bustle of a prosperous factory town is a thing of the far past.

A post office, three churches, a meat market, an ice cream shop, a pizza parlor, a garage, some newly constructed apartments, apartments in the closed elementary school, a youth baseball field, the American Legion Post,

Right: Rofin Company, Main Street, Clark Mills, 2010. *Courtesy of Marc R. Goldberg.*

Below: West Shore Railroad and Third Rail Interurban station, Clark Mills, circa 1925. The Rome and Clinton Railroad tracks are at right. *Courtesy of Mel and Evelyn Edwards.*

Ballet Dance Studio, Rofin and Rich Plan compose the commercial base of Clark Mills in 2011. A glove factory did turn out commercial gloves between 1960 and 1995 at facilities on New Street and Clinton Street.

In 1890, the Methodist Church began, the Church of the Annunciation started in 1910 and, between 1909 and 1978, the Gospel Chapel or Christian and Missionary Alliance Church also held services. The population changed after World War I, when several Lebanese and Syrian immigrants moved to Clark Mills.

Kirkland Senior Citizens/Police building, New Street, Clark Mills, 2010. *Courtesy of Marc R. Goldberg.*

One of the first American Legion posts in the country, No. 26, today owns and runs its chapter from the Arthur Hind Club off Main Street, formerly the recreation club for the plush company employees.

A fire department began in 1955 when Utica water was installed, providing hydrants and a sewer system (1956). A community band began in 1958 (now defunct), and in the 1960s, a senior citizens club met and now has a building that is shared with the Kirkland Town Police. Central Oneida County Volunteer Ambulance Corps started in a garage on White Street in 1970 and today occupies a complex on East South Street. It answers medical emergencies in the towns of Kirkland, Westmoreland and Whitestown and is a very busy outfit.

The two-family and single-family factory homes now are all owned by individuals, as Clark Mills is no longer a factory town. When Hind-Harrison operated, it supplied the water, electrical generation system and owned the streets.

Chapter 9

The Run to the Mohawk

After leaving Clark Mills, Oriskany Creek flows slowly north through the Town of Whitestown, sometimes called the "Mother of Towns." This was because, in 1788 when it formed, no other town existed west of here, so the rest of the New York State was in Whitestown. Shortly, though, other towns and counties were formed and taken away from Whitestown.

Hugh White and family from Middletown, Connecticut, settled in 1784 and bought a fourth of the three-thousand-acre Sadaqueda Patent. The town grew around the Village of Whitesboro, and within fifty years, the Erie Canal and the first railroads were built through the town. Now Whitestown is the largest town in the county, with nineteen thousand people in 2000, and includes four incorporated villages plus several hamlets.

PECKVILLE

About one and one-half miles north of Clark Mills is Peckville. A paper mill was built in 1844, and then a knitting mill used the building. In the 1880s, it was sold to Clark Mills Company, which removed machinery and left the structure to decay. Just north of the factory, the Peck family ran a wadding mill that employed several hands but was destroyed by fire. The business moved to Walesville and continued for a few years. Residents in the mid-1800s were John Peck, Erastus and Henry Loomis, Eli Peck and sons William and Frederick, who ran a store there where men collected each night for conversation.

Peckville had neither a saloon nor a church. It did have a tannery where John Parker made boots and shoes. Curtis White taught at a school that supposedly had over one hundred pupils. In 1915, the decaying knitting mill was torn down by Thomas F. McBride of Clinton. Today, Peckville hardly survives as a separate community except for the bridge, a farm and a few homes off Westmoreland Road.

WALESVILLE

The hamlet of Walesville is at an elevation of 465 feet and about a half mile downstream from Peckville. The hamlet can be traced back to May 1797 when Jonathan and Jerusha Wales of Windham, Connecticut, founded the settlement after a two-week journey by ox cart. Daughter Harriett was born in Connecticut, and son Henry and daughter Julia followed in Walesville. Jonathan Wales built a house in 1805 and engaged in "building up those interests which are of permanent value to the community." He farmed and raised stock, including fine horses. The Wales family and the Benjamin Buell families became connected when Alton Buell married Julia Wales. Some Smiths and Ladds also intermarried.

Henry Wales, born in Walesville in 1800, was the only son of Jonathan and Jerusha Wales. The family had high hopes for him and made sure he had the best. He graduated from nearby Hamilton College in 1820 with high honors, making the family proud. Tragedy struck soon, as Henry was lost in a shipwreck of the *Asp* on a voyage from Queenstown to Kingston in October 1820. Jonathan Wales ran a blacksmith shop and a tannery for morocco and buckskin leather. A gristmill to grind flour and meal started in the 1830 period. Oriskany Creek served as the source of this water power, and later, a wadding mill made batting. Halleck Mills and Company made shoulder pads for men's clothing.

Alton Buell had a cast-iron stove foundry in the 1840s, and Whitestown Manufacturing in 1851 employed seventy-five hands, using forty-five thousand pounds of wool a year to make tweeds and flannel. A cheese factory and a cotton mill also operated in the 1870s, but the most prominent was a paper mill, first opened in 1808 by Jonathan Wales and George Omlstead. Its products were writing paper, tissue paper and imitation leather for suitcases. After 1852, it was called Walter H. Olmstead & Company, makers of wrapping paper.

A general store, a post office, a schoolhouse and the Walesville Hotel were landmarks for years during Walesville's golden age. The hotel became known

Walesville Paper Mill, circa 1880. *Courtesy of Shirley Burtch.*

as Snyder's Hotel and supplied alcoholic beverages eagerly consumed by folks in the neighboring "dry" Town of Westmoreland. It burned in 1917, along with the paper mill in 1910. Halleck Mills burned in 1878, thus leaving little left of Walesville.

Combined with the railroad bypassing Walesville and the above fires, the decline of the community began, as the population of 115 in the 1870 census probably represented the high point for Walesville. The census again recorded 115 people in 1874, this time with 2 people of color. In that period, cast-iron stoves and men's suits were made there, but the post office was gone.

Dr. Wales Buell and his sister, Julia Buell, led a centennial celebration in 1897 with a dinner for forty-three with music provided by Bailey's Orchestra of Westmoreland. Dr. Buell practiced medicine in Utica, but since 1874, he had lived in the old Wales homestead in Walesville.

A Baptist church started in 1850, and it is now an apartment house on Westmoreland Road. It held worship services into the 1950s, and the Reverend Urban W. Newman was one of the last ministers. Newman had been the Town of Westmoreland supervisor and postmaster and served overseas in World War I.

Walesville in 2011 is a simple crossroads in the Town of Whitestown, minus all of its former activity and splendor. A flagpole and stone monument have marked the southwest area of the intersection since World War II. The

Walesville flag and World War II marker, Stone Road, 2010. *Courtesy of Marc R. Goldberg.*

bronze plaque reads, "In Enduring Love and Remembrance of Those Who Served Their Country from Walesville, New York." A stranger visiting today would not know that the bustling Walesville of the 1870s and 1880s ever existed. Its landscape, economy and appearance along Oriskany Creek have changed markedly since the mid-1800s.

A tragedy occurred here that made big news in local media in 1954. An air force F94C fighter plane crashed at the four corners, killing four people. Mrs. Doris Monroe was killed in her house, and Stanley, wife Florence and son Gary Phillips of Hecla were killed when a wing sheared off the plane and struck their automobile. The two air force lieutenants from Griffiss Air Force Base in Rome had parachuted to safety.

A major tributary joins Oriskany Creek just north of Walesville and south of the New York State Thruway. Dean's Creek starts around 1,230 feet above sea level in the northeastern section of the Town of Augusta north of Kimball

Oriskany dam and creek, view south of the Village of Oriskany, Valley Road, 2010. *Courtesy of Marc R. Goldberg.*

Road and west of Skyline Drive. Dean's Creek runs through rural land and the hamlets of Hecla and Westmoreland to join the Oriskany. James Dean, after whom the creek is named, came to this area in 1786 as a missionary to the Oneida Indians after being sent to live with Indians on the Susquehanna River at age eleven. He later attended Dartmouth College in Hanover, New Hampshire. Dean became a county judge and was given a two square mile land grant by the Oneida Indians. He also was a major in the army. He is considered the first settler in Westmoreland in 1786 on two miles square of land granted by the Oneida Indians. Early maps show this as "Dean's Patent."

COLEMAN'S MILLS

Our next community going downstream is called Coleman's Mills, and as the name suggests, it had the lumber mill of Appleton Hollister Coleman, the gristmill of Harry Wells, a cotton batting mill and a picking mill, all in the mid-1800s.

The bridge across the Oriskany is blocked to traffic, as the New York State Thruway caused changes to the roads in that area in the mid-1950s. Now Old Judd Road and New Judd Road exist there, and eight to ten houses, plus Domenicos Golf Course, makeup Coleman's Mills in 2011.

PLEASANT VALLEY

The area of Pleasant Valley remains a small settlement about one mile south of Oriskany on Valley Road. The Dexter Manufacturing Company was a large brick and stone factory, two hundred feet long, built in 1832. Dexter made wool cloth, shawls, tweeds, broad cloths and carpets. Its capital stock totaled $100,000, and Simon Newton Dexter took control of the firm in 1832. Besides the main mill two houses to dry the wool, a dye house and a wool house for storage made up the complex. Approximately 105 people, including men, women and children, were employed in 1840, working twelve hours a day. Connected to the mill were a day school, an evening school and a Sunday school. During the Civil War, it made army blankets, but it burned around 1880. The 1874 population was 87. Two of the old Dexter buildings, made of brick, are still in existence, along with a white Greek Revival house that has been remodeled into private homes on Valley Road.

Pleasant Valley, circa 1920. *Courtesy of Shirley Burtch.*

ORISKANY

The last village along Oriskany Creek is Oriskany, located on the former thirty-two thousand-acre Oriskany Patent, which was given to Thomas Wenham, George Clarke, Peter Schuyler, Peter Fauconnier, Robert Mompeson and others in 1705. These men all were prominent, influential and wealthy and stood in the good favor of the British Crown. The Fauconnier holdings passed to the DeLancey family in 1720.

As the DeLanceys were aggressive Loyalists, their land was taken in the Forfeiture Act of 1784 and put up for public sale. It was from this land that Gerrit G. Lansing, generally considered the founder of Oriskany, bought most of his four hundred acres. New York's first governor, George Clinton, bought part of Wenham's land for speculation in the 1790s.

Clarence J. Webster, writing in *A Touch of Gray* in 1974, said that "by 1800 Oriskany was on the move, on the main east-west travel route, old Indian trails had given way to roads on both sides of the Mohawk, but Oriskany's compelling asset was its creek, pretty and swift-flowing dropping 1000 feet between its source and its junction with the Mohawk."

Dam on Oriskany Creek, just south of the Village of Oriskany, Valley Road, 2010. *Courtesy of Marc R. Goldberg.*

Webster continued, "Land sold for $3.00 per acre along the creek and 50 cents to $1.00 back from the water. Water was everything—to turn a wheel, to ensure the growth of crops on wilderness soil, and to sustain life for struggling settlers."

An explanation about the name "Oriska" is needed. It was the Oneida Indian name for a village there before the Revolutionary War. The Indian name for Oriskany meant "River of Nettles." In some places, it appears as "Oriske." The "n" and "y" were added to make "Oriskany" and to supposedly to clear up confusion at the post office.

In 1784, Ephraim Webster first settled in Oriskany but did not stay too long. Abraham Van Eps arrived in 1795 and established a small trading post in what is now Oriskany. Colonel Gerrit Lansing served as a lieutenant in the Revolutionary War and served under General Alexander Hamilton at Yorktown. He built a sawmill and gristmill in the 1810s. By 1840, Oriskany had sixty dwellings, one woolen mill, the Erie Canal and the railroad.

The Oriskany Manufacturing Company was started in 1810 by Dr. Seth Capron (1763–1835) and others as the first woolen factory in the United States. Capron was an officer in the Revolutionary War and served as an aide to General Washington. His mother was M. Eunice Mann, sister of famous nineteenth-century educator Horace Mann. Stockholders along with Capron were prominent and important men of the period: DeWitt Clinton, Stephen Van Rensselaer and Gerrit Lansing. Initial capital was $200,000. In 1818, the mill wove the first woolen yarn ever made on a power loom in the United States. The three-story brick and stone structure became a landmark in downtown Oriskany and was the site for the Waterbury Felt mill. Oriskany Manufacturing Company went out of business in 1855.

An inadequate supply of local wool caused merino sheep to be imported during the War of 1812. The sheep had been kept on Dr. Capron's Deerfield farm and others'. Capron started the Mount Merino Sheep Association here. In 1825, Capron left for Orange County in the lower Hudson Valley and established the town of Walden on the Wallkill.

By 1851, S. Newton Dexter had bought the woolen mill, which suffered during the Panic of 1857 and closed in 1858. A.B. Buell of Westmoreland purchased the location and established the Buell and Halleck Malleable Iron Company, which made malleable iron and brass castings. Later it became Buell and Merriman Malleable Iron Company and made some farm implements and frames for Remington typewriters in Ilion. Buell also had a woolen mill side by side with Waterbury Felt for a short time.

Oriskany Malleable Iron was originally on the Waterbury site but later moved across the Erie Canal to the east bank of Oriskany Creek. It turned out castings for over one hundred years until it went bankrupt and closed in 1969. When possible, castings were stamped with a small outline of the Oriskany Monument.

Henry Waterbury in 1878 brought his Rensselaerville Woolen Mill from Rensselaerville, New York, to the Malleable Iron/woolen mill building. The firm's name was H. Waterbury and Sons Company and doubled in size in 1887. The mill in Rensselaerville suffered from a lack of skilled labor and was too far from main transportation lines. The Oriskany mill sat a few feet from the Erie Canal and a few yards from the New York Central Railroad, thus solving that problem.

Papermaker felts began to be made in the United States, and they consisted of a flat strip of felt that prepared paper for loft drying. Henry Waterbury and his wife, Mary, devised a way of joining the ends of this woven fabric to form an endless belt. The manufactured felts were made to order for the customers. The raw wool came from around the world for sorting, washing, blending and carding. The woven felts become an endless belt that goes to the fulling section of the mill where the felts are washed and fulled to proper

Waterbury mill and Erie Canal, Village of Oriskany, circa 1900. *Courtesy of Oriskany Museum.*

dimensions, causing the matting and clinging of wool fibers, which provides the porous quality to allow water to be removed from the paper stock.

Waterbury Felt has a long history and still operates at the corner of State Route 69 and River Street. This site has been an industrial one since the 1810s when what is believed to be the first woolen mill in the country was erected. Waterbury employed 160 people in 1976. Peter Earl owns the Waterbury complex now.

Public schools began in 1810 in a log cabin at Utica and Cider Streets, and later, a brick building on Utica Street was built. In 1892, a wooden school was removed from the Utica Street site, and a new brick school was constructed. This was called the "Union School" and was a common name in the state for village schools prior to centralization, which began in the 1920s. Oriskany became a central district in 1931. Some of the one-room schools from the towns of Whitestown, Floyd, Marcy and Rome, plus the Oriskany village union school district, composed the new "Oriskany Central School." At 1312 Utica Street, the new kindergarten through twelfth-grade school was built in 1933, with additions being attached in 1950, 1953 and 1970. As student population continued to increase, the N.A. Walbran Elementary School at 8610 State Route 69 was constructed in 1960 and added to four years later. Still a separate district today, Oriskany Central has eight hundred students.

By the 1870s, Oriskany had seen much commercial activity: a tobacco factory in 1833, a gristmill, two blacksmiths, a foundry, a wagon shop, three hotels, a private school, a post office, two tin shops and a public school.

Similar to the other Oriskany Valley communities, organized religion of four churches began with the Presbyterian Society in 1831 and became the Waterbury Memorial Presbyterian Church after the family of Henry Waterbury provided funds to build the current edifice at 909 Utica Street in 1901. St. Peter's Episcopal Church started in 1830 on Utica Street and closed in 1996. A Welsh Calvinistic Methodist Church on Utica Street began in 1840 but closed in 1921. St. Stephen's Roman Catholic Church opened in 1928 on Dexter Avenue, but it now has ceased services.

Summit Park operated overlooking Oriskany Creek between 1897 and 1926 in the days when mass transit in the form of trolley cars was still popular and viable. The Utica Belt Railroad owned it and laid tracks from Utica through Yorkville and Whitesboro to the park on the east side of the Creek. Some kettle holes from glaciations in Summit Park remain. The park entertained thousands of Utica-area folks with a casino, an ice cream bar, a soda fountain, row boats, canoes and swimming on the Oriskany, an observatory, a baseball field, a picnic area, large bands for dancing, a quarter mile track, a merry-go-round and minstrel shows and vaudeville during the summer months. Admission was ten cents at first, and the whole family could enjoy a pleasant summer day for little money. Although closed in 1926, a brief revival occurred in the late 1950s, but it proved unsuccessful, and now the land is vacant.

The Village of Oriskany incorporated in 1914 and has a mayor and four trustees to handle affairs of village. The streets, a fire department (which started in 1900), a police department and trash and garbage removal are other services. It covers 0.8 square miles.

Oriskany is the site of the New York State Eastern Star Home, which was dedicated September 1916. It began in Waterville at the Osborne home in 1907. The former Waterbury Homestead mansion at 1400 Utica Street was acquired and is now a chapel (1933); several other buildings offer different levels of assisted living and nursing home care. In 2005, a Victorian pavilion for community use was erected, and the Day Care Center continues to serve the area with an emphasis for students with dyslexia.

The Trinkaus family of four brothers (Stonie, Anthony, William and Andy) opened Trinkaus Manor in 1946 in the former Waterbury homestead on Route 69. The thousands of Christmas lights and decorations brought

Trinkaus Manor—a popular restaurant in Oriskany after World War II. *Courtesy of Mel and Evelyn Edwards.*

fame to the restaurant and became a "must-see" each December for area residents and visitors alike. An adjacent motel opened in 1960, but a fire unfortunately destroyed the restaurant on April 5, 1992.

Oriskany village residents and the Village of Oriskany in 1997 donated money and erected the Oriskany Museum at 420 Utica Street in Trinkaus Park. It holds items about the August 6, 1777 Battle of Oriskany, village artifacts and historical items and memorabilia from the USS *Oriskany*, which was named after the village in 1950.

David Pitkin was the first curator and helped start the collection in 1967 through the Battle of Oriskany Historical Society, which was housed in the village library at 806 Utica Street. Pitkin was also a history teacher at Oriskany High School. Later, Robert Heeley was the curator and did much to establish the new museum in Trinkaus Park and to organize the collection. The Village of Oriskany now provides funding along with former sailors who served on the USS *Oriskany*. The park has an A-4E Skyhawk fighter plane and other artifacts, such as the anchor and a bell from the carrier. The park itself was dedicated in May 1992, but the bell didn't arrive until September 1995.

The USS *Oriskany* was in service until 1976. Tragically, forty-four crewmen were lost in a fire on the carrier on October 26, 1966, in the Gulf of Tonkin during the Vietnam War. The Essex-class USS *Oriskany* was decommissioned in 1976 after service in Korea and Vietnam and now rests near Pensacola, Florida. In mothballs for thirty years, the "Mighty O" was laid to rest as an artificial reef in the Gulf of Mexico on May 17, 2006.

In addition to the Oriskany Museum, the Battle of Oriskany Historical Society also does much to keep Oriskany's history alive for current residents.

Oriskany Museum,
420 Utica Street,
Oriskany, 2010
*Courtesy of Marc R.
Goldberg.*

This aqueduct, pictured in 2010, carried Erie Canal over the Oriskany in Oriskany prior to 1915, when the Barge Canal was built. It is located next to the State Route 69 Bridge. *Courtesy of Marc R. Goldberg.*

Its projects include adding forty-two more names of World War II veterans on a plaque in the high school, placing plastic flag holders on graves of veterans and updating lists of veterans in the Oriskany Cemetery.

Population-wise, by 1860, 711 lived in the village; 584 plus 1 person of color in 1874. The Village of Oriskany had 1,459 residents in the 2000 census.

The Erie Canal arrived in Oriskany in 1819 when the Rome to Utica section opened. At first, an aqueduct was built to take the canal over the Oriskany on top of a dam. Around 1840, the aqueduct—whose stone foundation pillars of the aqueduct survive today just south of the State Route 69 bridge—was built over Oriskany Creek. The canal was filled in 1918 after the new Barge Canal opened with a wider and deeper channel about one mile north of the village.

Community pride arose during "Oriskany Days," which were celebrated in the 1970s, and the last one was on the bicentennial of the Battle of Oriskany, which occurred in 1977. Additionally, a new library (1988) and a fire station (1969) provide needed community services.

Old Erie Canal aqueduct in Oriskany, which was still used prior to 1915. *Courtesy of Shirley Burtch.*

The Roux Wire Die Works, founded by German-born Adrian P. Roux, operated in Oriskany between 1936 and 1988 on Utica Street in a building that is now gone. It made high quality diamond dies. In 2011, Madden Concrete operates on the 1880s site of a former malleable iron works. 84 Lumber on Route 69 and Steel Treaters on Furnace Street provide some employment to Oriskany residents. Steel Treaters processes both ferrous and nonferrous metals for local customers.

For the past half dozen years, Oriskany has had a monthly newspaper the *0*, which reports Oriskany happenings at school, churches and sports events. David Fay sells display ads and runs the periodical.

Through the histories of the villages and hamlets and the explanations of the changes, the advances, the tragedies and the triumphs, the social, economic and cultural milieu of the Oriskany Creek Valley comes to life. Today's residents and readers can realize that no area stays the same through the years but rather experiences flux and tension to adjust. Likewise, the common threads of the several communities reinforce that fact that most have similar organizations, establishments, businesses and religious groups. While differences in the communities exist, more facets are familiar and are in almost predictable patterns. Each has progressed from remote, forested, self-sufficient hamlets to villages dependent on a vast worldwide economy for survival and sustenance.

Chapter 10

Economy of the Valley

The economy of the Oriskany Valley developed in virtual isolation during the early years, between the 1780s and the 1820s. Cutting down trees for farmland and materials for houses and barns created a need for sawmills, which were built on creeks. Farmers needed gristmills to grind the grain into meal or flour for cooking and to feed cattle. Ashes were made into potash for fertilizer and to make soap.

The early settlers from New England brought their flocks with them, including cattle for the dairy and oxen for the wooden plow. By 1789, a few horses were brought to Clinton, and Moses Foote, an early horse owner, had one stolen by Indians, according to tradition. Other early Clinton horse owners were William Carpenter and Nathan Marsh in 1789.

Each hamlet needed a cooper to make barrels, a blacksmith to shoe horses and to make small tools, a harness maker to fashion reins and tack for horses, carpenters, cobblers to make shoes and boots and tanneries, which used hemlock bark to process hides.

Early factories in the valley employed men to work at carding mills, cotton factories, trip hammer shops, malleable ironworks and forges. Small farms were the norm, using the farmer and his family for labor. Gradually, farmers hired hands to help during the harvest and then to work year-round.

Wages in the Oriskany Valley were minimal amounts in the 1850s, according to the U.S. census. Some examples for the Town of Marshall are: $12.00 per month for a farmhand with board; $0.75 a day for a laborer with board; $1.00 a day for a laborer without board; $1.50 per

Hind & Harrison Plush Mill, Clark Mills, Main Street, circa 1965. *Courtesy of Clinton Historical Society.*

day for a carpenter without board; and $1.00 weekly for a domestic female with board.

For the Town of Augusta in the 1870s, wages were as follows: thirty-three dollars per month for common hard labor; thirty-five dollars per month for a farmhand; ten dollars per month for a woman doing household work; eighteen dollars per month for a woman in a factory; sixty dollars a month for a male teacher; and forty dollars per month for a female teacher.

The Erie Canal was the longest canal in the United States, some 363 miles long, 4 feet deep and 40 feet wide. The politician most responsible for the canal was DeWitt Clinton, New York's governor who oversaw the bonding and construction, which began in Rome on July 4, 1817.

The Erie Canal opened in the central section through Oneida County in October 1819. No steam shovels or bulldozers were used—just pick axes, shovels, stump pullers and lots of human sweat and muscle. Railroads followed closely on the heels of the canals by 1837 and changed the transportation system completely. Rail competition marked the end of viable canal traffic, but in 1918, the new Barge Canal opened, providing jobs in construction and making transport less expensive for bulk goods, such as wheat, coal and oil.

Chenango Canal lock on Valley Road, Town of Madison, 2010. *Courtesy of Marc R. Goldberg.*

The Barge Canal construction cut a new channel separate from the old Erie Canal and used the Mohawk, Seneca and Oswego Rivers for much of the way between Cohoes and Buffalo. The wider barges required a deeper and wider canal. Pleasure boats use the Barge Canal today, which was renamed the Erie Canal a few years ago.

After the success of the Erie Canal, in 1825, every section of the state wanted a canal. Residents of the Oriskany and the Chenango Valleys were no exception and lobbied hard—eventually successfully, because, in the late 1820s and early 1830s, there was state money to build a canal between Utica and Binghamton.

The Chenango Canal was authorized by the state legislature in 1833, and Rome's John B. Jervis was appointed the chief engineer. The Omnibus Canal Bill provided funding, and the cost in the end totaled $2,316, 816—about twice what the original estimates were. The new canal promised to bring cheaper anthracite coal from Pennsylvania mines to the center of the New York and take Chenango Valley farm products to market.

The new canal had a width of forty feet at the top and twenty-six feet at the bottom with a depth of four feet. A ten-foot-wide towpath ran down one side for the mules and horses, and a berme on the other side served as a bank. The Chenango Canal had 116 locks, 52 culverts, 19 aqueducts to take the canal over creeks and rivers and 162 bridges. The boats traveled about four miles per hour. Some classes of the boats were packet boats, scows, lakers and bullheads for freight.

A reservoir system of small lakes provided water at the summit level. John B. Jervis developed this unique method to provide water at the summit through

Chenango Canal
lock on Valley Road,
Town of Madison,
2010. *Courtesy of Marc
R. Goldberg.*

Bouckville, which is 706 feet above the Erie Canal. Jervis used a rain gauge to determine that 40 percent of rainfall in Eaton, Hamilton and Bouckville was retained in the lakes (reservoirs), which would be a reliable supply to the canal summit that straddles the watersheds for the Mohawk and the Chenango Rivers. The summit level ran from just south of Solsville to just north of Hamilton. Coal, hay and dairy products shipped north; lumber, iron ore, lime and limestone went south. Hops and apple cider were also transported. The canal never made a profit from tolls. Some businesses were ruined because the streams dammed or diverted to the feeder system and could no longer power local mills. Numerous court actions occurred, especially in the Solsville area, where the canal caused much disruption of business.

Many Scotch and Irish immigrants did back-breaking labor with pick and shovel to build the locks and other facilities between Utica and Binghamton for eleven dollars per month. Labor difficulties ensued on the Deansboro section when workers went on strike. The workers lived in shantytowns along the route, and the laborers between Oriskany Falls and Deansboro staged a rebellion. This was referred to as Paddy's Rebellion, so the state militia was called from Cassety Hollow (Oriskany Falls) and marched with flags flying and drums beating against the workers. The militia was met by some of the workers' wives, who had made weapons by stuffing rocks into their cotton stockings. The troubles soon subsided.

Marshall historian Dorothy McConnell relates how the Reverend Samuel Miller visited a shanty where the Irish workers lived in poverty. The parents and a little boy each had a spoon in hand taking soup out of a pan. Every now and then the pig would come up and slush his snout into the boy's soup for his share. The little boy would hit him over the nose with his spoon and drive him away to the amusement of his parents.

The canal did have some benefits between 1836 and its closing in 1878. It did open up the Chenango and Oriskany Valleys, making transportation cheaper and quicker for farmers and merchants alike. The cost to transport goods to Albany used to take nine to thirteen days at $1.25 per one hundred pounds by horse and wagon. After 1837, it took four days and $0.25 per one hundred pounds.

Former Clinton historian Phil Munson told this delightful canal anecdote,

> *The first lock tender for several locks in Clinton was Samuel Foote, well-known as "Uncle Sam." "Uncle Sam" was not a little vain of his office as lock tender, and was noted for his excitable temperament, which the "boys" about the village were fond of stirring up.*
>
> *Late one Saturday evening several of said boys arranged to meet at the lock below the village (east) and blow a horn to call "Uncle Sam" to his official duty. He, supposing the first boat had arrived, responded in great haste, puffing and wheezing to "get there" in time to lock the boat through. But alas! There was no boat in sight. The boys had secreted themselves behind the bank and were fully repaid for their pains by listening to "Uncle Sam's" stentorian anathemas, for giving him such a tiresome chase for naught.*

Inns, taverns, stores, warehouses and forwarding agents sprang up, bringing prosperity to villages and hamlets along the route. Oriskany Falls and Clinton are both good examples of that.

The Chenango Canal traffic declined slowly but steadily after the continued successes of the Erie Canal and when the railroad spanned the Oriskany Valley by 1870. Tolls collected never paid what it cost to build and maintain. Political pressures combined with charges of mismanagement, competition from the railroads and fraud helped nail the canal's coffin shut. The locks were in poor repair, water was low at times and the public sentiment went against keeping it open, so it officially closed after the 1877 season.

Few passengers used the Chenango, as freight became the main cargo. Railroads followed closely on the heels of the seasonal canals, causing the latter to decline in importance. The canal land was sold to contiguous property owners or municipalities through which it passed. Even the bridges, stone from some of the locks and all iron work was auctioned off. In many villages, streets were built over the canal bed, such as Chenango Avenue in Clinton.

Today between Deansboro and Solsville, several locks of the old Chenango Canal are still visible. Local-quarried limestone was used for the walls, many of which still stand.

The state did retain five miles of the canal in the Bouckville area to receive water by feeders from seven artificial lakes in the town of Eaton that provide water to this day for the Erie Canal. See Chapter 1 for a full explanation.

The plank road era began after 1849 and ended in the 1870s for this area. The plank roads were built and maintained by stock companies that laid cedar plank on beams for the road surface. Hard to maintain and to keep in good repair, the roads' keepers charged tolls at three-mile intervals to pay for the upkeep. The macadam roads movement for "good roads" kicked in around the 1890s in the Oriskany Valley, with State Route 26 between Oriskany Falls and Rome being one of the first paved state roads by the 1911 period. Some local villages started to pave roads around 1910. The messy and nasty dirt roads eventually gave way to pavement, either concrete or macadam.

Just as every village wanted a canal in the 1830s, in the 1850s and 1860s, every community wanted a railroad, and most of them were willing to pay part of the cost with public tax money. The Utica, Clinton & Binghamton Railroad was formed by Othniel S. Williams, a prominent Clinton lawyer, civic leader, judge, Hamilton College treasurer and businessman. In early 1866, after town

NYO&W train station and post office in Clark Mills, Mill Street, circa 1920. Clark Mills United Methodist Church is at the far left. *Courtesy of Clinton Historical Society.*

governments and individuals put up money to buy stock, construction began and the first train arrived in Clinton on September 3, 1866. Paralleling the canal from Utica to Solsville, the towns and some villages bought stock in the railroad to entice it to build through the town. The Town of Kirkland held stock until the mid-1940s and received dividends many years.

Extended to Randallsville by 1870, the UC&B met the newly formed New York Oswego & Midland. The railroad seriously affected economic prospects of the Chenango Canal. Now coal and copper ingots went to Rome, and sugar and stone went south. Every town had its coal dealers and coal trestles adjacent to the tracks. The corporate story of the rails through the Oriskany Valley is a complex and complicated tale of mergers, bankruptcies and various owners and leasers until the New York Ontario & Western Railroad ended in bankruptcy in March 1957.

The Rome & Clinton Railroad connected Rome, the copper city, through Clark Mills, Westmoreland and Bartlett, to Clinton between 1872 and 1957. The Town of Kirkland held $20,000 in stock, which it sold to NYO&W in 1946, the year the R&C Railroad ended.

In the Oriskany and Big Creek Valleys, hops, corn, wheat, barley, string beans, dairy, peas and apples (Northern spies) were main crops. Kirkland became a major fruit-growing town by the 1850s; apples were also grown in Deansboro into the 1980s on Brooks Road. Soybeans are a relatively recent crop.

NYO&W engine 272. *Courtesy of Clinton Historical Society.*

Town of Marshall farm, "Dunrovin," Shanley Road, 2009. *Courtesy of Marc R. Goldberg.*

Harvest time in rural areas of the Oriskany Valley required laborers in addition to family members to pick the crops. The farm wife had to cook large meals and lodge the harvesters each year in August and September. The nature of the laborers changed through the years.

Between 1900 and the 1930s, Polish and Italian immigrants who lived in Utica or elsewhere picked the crops and lived on farms in the country for the harvest season. After World War II and in 1950s, black migrants from Belle Glade, Florida, and other southern states came north in the summer to pick crops and "lived" in crude camps owned by farmers. Many were paid in coupons or tickets, instead of cash, which could be used in local stores.

Top farmers in the 1930s to 1950s were Murk Wester in Kirkland on Bristol Road and Claude Hinman, who lived just north of Deansboro in Kirkland. Several large dairy farms continue today throughout the Oriskany Valley.

In Waterville, Kirkland and Marshall in 2011, dairy farming remains a major industry with several attractive dairy farms that raise feed for the cows and send unprocessed milk to various plants. Some Mennonite farm families have moved here from Pennsylvania since the 1980s and bought out local farmers. This has kept much farmland and many farmhands in business. A few large farmers hire Latin American immigrants to work in the dairies.

Conclusion

The Oriskany and Big Creek Valleys in the future will probably see a decrease in the farm sector if current trends continue. Mills and factories will never see anything like the golden years of the mid-1800s, as retail, education and medical facilities have drawn more employees during the past fifty years. Fishermen will still find great spots to catch those brown trout, and the various villages will still rely on the creek's aquifer for drinking water and for outflows from waste water plants.

Technology has rendered Big and Oriskany Creeks basically obsolete as a power source in today's high-tech world. The former role of turning waterwheels and burrstones no longer prevails, as electricity has replaced water power. Recreational and municipal uses dominate today.

What will the valleys look like and be like in one hundred years can only be imagined with present trends of climate warming, computers and microcircuitry. Nearby wind turbines in the Town of Madison might be a harbinger of more to come.

While the Oriskany and Big Creek Valleys' natural features remain nearly as they were in the early settler years of the late 1780s and 1790s, modern technology and science and the Internet have caused changes in how people live, work and play. People can't change the setting, but they have been adept at adapting themselves to technology advances and inventions to seek prosperity and a good life. That drive for success should not diminish in the Oriskany and Big Creek Valleys.

Appendix

ELEVATIONS

Area	Feet Above Sea Level
Oriskany Creek, at source in the Town of Stockbridge near Prospect Hill	1,490
Solsville	1,125
Lyon's Mills	1,060
Oriskany Falls	960
Deansboro	795
Farmer's Mills	650
Franklin Springs	620
Clinton-College Street Bridge	575
Village Park	583
Norton Avenue Bridge	550
Kirkland	533
Clark Mills	520
Peckville	465
Walesville	478
Coleman's Mills	460
Oriskany	424
Oriskany Creek at Mohawk River	410
Big Creek at source in the Town of Marshall	1,454

Waterville	1,230
Forge Hollow	980
At confluence of Big Creek and Oriskany Creek just northeast of Deansboro	780

POPULATION IN THE ORISKANY AND BIG CREEK VALLEYS

Town	Year 1800	1850	1900	1950	2000
Augusta	1,598	2,271	2,029	1,933	1,966
Kirkland	*600	3,421	4,852	6,164	10,138
Madison	*300	2,483	2,250	2,400	2,801
Marshall	*1,000	2,115	1,804	1,606	2,127
Sangerfield	1,143	2,371	2,440	2,143	2,610
Whitestown	4,214	6,810	6,235	12,686	17,382

*These are estimates, as Kirkland and Marshall in 1800 were in the Town of Paris population data; Madison was in the Town of Hamilton in the 1800 census. Also listed in the 1800 census were 42 slaves in Augusta; 155 slaves in Paris, which contained Marshall and Kirkland; and 155 slaves in Whitestown, which contained Walesville and the village of Oriskany.

Bibliography

Atlas of Oneida County. Philadelphia, PA: D.G. Beers and Company, 1874.

Beetle, David H. *Along the Oriskany*. Rochester, NY: Heindl and Son, 1947.

Bogan, Jim. *Big Creek Valley*. Homely Ways Press, 2003.

Chenango Canal.org.

Clear Waters (Fall 2009).

Clinton Courier.

Commemorative Program 190th Anniversary of the Battle of Oriskany. Oriskany, NY: August 4–6, 1967.

Cookinham, Henry J. *History of Oneida County*. 2 vols. Chicago, IL: S.J. Clarke Publishing Co., 1912.

Darlington, James W. "Peopling the Post-Revolutionary New York Frontier." *New York History* (October 1993).

Deane, S.N. *A New England Pioneer Among the Oneida Indians, Life of James Dean*. Northampton Historical Society, 1926.

Diet for a Small Lake. 2nd ed. New York State Federation of Lake Associations, Inc., 2009.

Disturnell, J. *A Gazeteer of the State of New York*. N.p., 1842.

Durant, Samuel. *History of Oneida County*. New York and Philadelphia, PA: Everts and Fariss, 1878.

Ellis, David M. *Landlords and Farmers in the Hudson-Mohawk Region 1790–1850*. Ithaca, NY: Cornell University Press, 1946.

———. *The Upper Mohawk Valley*. Woodland Hills, CA: Oneida Historical Society, 1982.

First Annual Oriskany Days Celebration. Oriskany, NY: July 31–August 2, 1971.

French, J.H., *Gazeteer of New York State.* N.p., 1860.

Fultonhistory.com.

Gridley, A.D. *History of the Town of Kirkland.* New York: Hurd and Houghton, 1874.

Hedrick, Ulysses P. *A History of Agriculture in the State of New York.* New York State Agriculture Society, 1933. Reprint, New York: Hill & Wang, 1966.

Helmer, William F. *Ontario & Western.* Berkeley, CA: Howell-North, 1959.

A History of the Eastern Star Home, Oriskany, N.Y., Oriskany, NY: Oriskany Museum, n.d.

Jennings, Francis, ed. *History and Culture of Iroquois Diplomacy.* Syracuse, NY: Syracuse University Press, 1985.

Jones, Pomroy. *Annals and Recollections of Oneida County.* Rome, NY: 1851.

Kelly, Joe. *USS Oriskany Fact Book.* Utica, NY: Good Times Publishing, 1997.

Kelly, Virginia. *The History of Oneida County.* Oneida County, NY: 1977.

Kessler, Paul M. *Mohawk Discovering the Valley of the Crystals.* Kessler Family, 2008.

Klein, Milton M. *The Empire State, A History of New York.* Ithaca, NY: Cornell University Press, 2001.

Larkin, F. Daniel. *New York State Canals.* Fleischmanns, NY: Purple Mountain Press, 1998.

Mapquest.com.

McConnell, Dorothy. *Echoes of Forge Hollow.* Deansboro, NY: Marshall Historical Society, 1996.

McFee, Michele A. *Limestone Locks & Overgrowth.* Fleischmanns, NY: Purple Mountain Press, 1993.

New Century Atlas of Oneida County. Philadelphia, PA: New Century Map Co., 1907.

Oneida County New York State 1800 Federal Population Census Schedule. Cambridge, MA: Ralph V. Wood Jr., 1962.

Roots in the Hollow, Life in the Falls. Brookfield, NY: Worden Press, 1989.

Smith, James H., ed. *History of Chenango & Madison Counties,* Syracuse, NY: D. Mason & Co., 1880.

Solms, Jennifer G.F., and Paula A. Schoonmaker, eds. *Country Roads, Madison County's Heritage: A Resource for the Future.* Wampsville, NY: Madison County Planning Board, 1976.

Spafford, H.G. *Gazeteer of New York State.* N.p., 1813.

———. *Gazeteer of New York State.* N.p., 1824.

Summit Park. Oriskany, NY: Oriskany Museum, n.d.

Taibi, John. *Rails Along the Oriskany.* Fleischmanns, NY: Purple Mountain Press, 2003

Third Annual Oriskany Day Celebration. N.p., August 5–7, 1983.

Torrey, E. Fuller. *Frontier Justice, the Rise & Fall of the Loomis Gang.* Utica, NY: North Country Books, 1992.

Town of Sangerfield Bicentennial 1795–1995. Utica, NY: Waterville Historical Society and Oneida BOCES, 1995.

Towpaths, Turnpikes, and Towns. New Hartford, NY: Oneida County BOCES, 1985.

Utica Daily Press.

Wager, Daniel F., *Oneida County.* Boston, MA: Boston History Co., 1896.

Waterville Times.

White, Donald. *Exploring 200 Years of Oneida County History.* Utica, NY: Oneida County Historical Society, 1998.

Williams, Emily, and Helen Cardamone, *Canal Country.* Self-published, 1982.

Williams, Richard L., ed. *Farms and Barns of Kirkland, New York.* Clinton, NY: Clinton Historical Society, 2008.

———. *Kirkland since 1827.* Clinton, NY: Clinton Historical Society, 2002.

Index

B

Barton, Clara 98
Barton Hose Company 85, 87
Bogan, Jim 80, 135
Brant, Joseph 39
Bristol-Myers-Squibb Company 90
Brothertown Indians 35, 36, 37,
    38, 80, 81, 83, 93
Bryne Dairy 103
Buell, Alton 110

C

Capron, Seth 116
Cassety, Thomas 68, 70
Central Oneida County Volunteer
    Ambulance Corps 108
Chenango Canal 6, 9, 10, 11, 12,
    13, 14, 15, 16, 26, 57, 62, 63,
    68, 70, 71, 83, 91, 125, 127,
    128, 129, 135
Chenango River 11, 25, 46, 62,
    126
Cherry Valley Turnpike 46, 47, 48,
    52, 63

Cleveland, Erastus 62, 63
Clinton hematite 22, 90, 94
Clinton Metallic Paint Company
    90, 95
Covidien 13, 74
Coxe Patent 44
C.W. Clark Memorial Library 71

D

Dean, James 35, 44, 113, 135
Dean, John 36, 81
Dean's Creek 19, 112, 113
Dean, Thomas 36, 81, 83
Delaware, Lackawanna and West-
    ern 55
Dexter Manufacturing Company
    114
Douglas Memorial Park 71
Dugway 22, 25, 85, 92

E

Eastman, George 56
Erie Canal 6, 10, 16, 109, 116, 117,
    121, 124, 125, 126, 127, 128

F

Flora Temple 53, 54
Foote, Moses 89, 123

G

gold cure 100

H

Hageman, W.A. 105
Herkimer, Nicholas 39, 40
Hind, Arthur 105, 108
Hinman, Claude 84, 130
Hinman, Grove 63, 66, 84
hockey 91, 100
Hopkins, Dr. Samuel 27
hops 48, 49, 50, 51, 74, 80, 84, 88,
    126, 129
Huddle, the 46, 48, 52

I

Indium Company 91

J

James Rhodes Company 91, 95, 96
Jervis, John B. 125, 126
Johnson, William 33

K

Kirkland Bird Club 31
Kirkland, Samuel 31, 34, 35, 43,
    44, 99, 100
Knox, John Jay 69

L

Lansing, Gerrit G. 115, 116
lithia water 90, 93, 95
Loomis Gang 51, 55, 137
Lyon's Mills 68, 76, 133

M

Maccabees 87
Madison Lake 16, 63, 64
Miller, Isaac 80
Mohawk River 7, 9, 17, 20, 21, 34,
    39, 40, 41, 43, 46, 62, 126,
    133
Musical Museum 88

N

New York Ontario & Western Rail-
    road 27, 66, 76, 83, 91, 129
New York Oswego & Midland Rail-
    road 129
New York State Department of
    Environmental Conservation
    12, 27, 28, 30, 104
New York State Eastern Star Home
    119, 136

O

Occom, Samson 36
Old Moyer Road 41
Oneidas 33, 34, 35, 36, 37, 38, 39,
    40, 43, 44, 62, 68, 89, 99,
    113, 116
Oriskany Museum 5, 120, 136

P

Paddy's Rebellion 126
Pitarresi, John 6, 27

R

Riverhawk Company 91
Rock City 22
Rofin Company 90, 106
Rome & Clinton Railroad 102, 129
Rome Turney Radiator 106
Root, Elihu 98
Root Glen 19, 31, 32

Root, Oren 26, 30, 31
Rural Art Society 31

S

Sangerfield Driving Park 58
Sanger, Jedediah 45, 46, 48
Sanger Mansion 59
Sanger, William Cary 59
Seneca Turnpike 34, 41, 91, 101, 102, 104
Smith, Peter 44, 68
Stigmatines 59, 60
St. Leger, Barry 39, 40
Stockbridge Indians 37, 38
Stockwell 45, 48
Stone Congregational Church 77, 78
Summit Park 118, 136

T

Tassel Hill 17, 18, 60, 85
Tower, Reuben, I 57
Tower, Reuben, II 57
Treaty of Fort Stanwix 36, 43
Trinkaus Manor 119
Tucker, George 71, 78
Tyler's Mills 62

U

USS *Oriskany* 120, 136
Utica, Chenango & Susqehanna Valley Railroad 54
Utica, Clinton and Binghamton Railroad 83, 91

V

Van Eps, Abraham 116

W

Wales family 110
Waterbury, Henry 117, 118

Wester, Murk 130
White, Hugh 109
Whitestown 51, 62, 80, 108, 109, 110, 111, 118, 134
Willett, Marinus 40
Williams, Othniel S. 128

About the Author

Richard L. Williams is a Clinton native who graduated in 1962 from Syracuse University with a history degree and from the State University at Albany in 1963 with a master's degree in social studies education. After serving two years as an army officer, he taught history and economics first at LaFayette High School, LaFayette, New York, and then at Whitesboro Senior High School, Marcy, New York. In 1980, he became vice-principal at Whitesboro, a position he held until his retirement in 1995.

In his hometown, Williams has been active with the Clinton Fire Department, the Methodist church and the Clinton Historical Society, serving the society as president in 1972–1974 and 1999–2004. He was also on the Village of Clinton Board of Trustees between 1975 and 1987 when he was elected mayor. He held that office until 1997.

Other books Williams has edited or written include the *Clinton American Revolution Bicentennial Committee Booklet* (1976), *Clinton's Bicentennial, a Picture History* (1987), *Kirkland Since 1827* (2002) and *Farms & Barns of Kirkland, New York* (2008).

Additionally, Williams has contributed local history articles to the *Clinton Courier* since 1985 and served as administrator at the Oneida County Historical Society for five months in 1997.

Visit us at
www.historypress.net